金原瑞人
My Favorites

Ernest Hemingway

The Snows of Kilimanjaro
The Short Happy Life of Francis Macomber

キリマンジャロの雪
フランシス・マカンバーの短く幸せな生涯
アーネスト・ヘミングウェイ

青灯社

Copyright © All rights outside U.S., Hemingway Foreign Rights Trust.
Used by permission of the Hemingway Foreign Rights Trust
through Japan UNI Agency, Inc.

まえがき

1. アーネスト・ヘミングウェイの短編ふたつ

　この英語の注釈シリーズもこれで5冊目。今回は、アメリカの20世紀を代表する作家のひとりアーネスト・ヘミングウェイの短編、The Snows of Kilimanjaro と The Short Happy Life of Francis Macomber を取り上げてみた。両方とも、同時期に書かれている。そしてどちらも、アフリカにハンティングにやってきた白人夫婦の物語で、どちらも最後が衝撃的で、じつに切ない。また短編小説としても驚くほど完成度が高く、何度読み返しても、感動が薄れない。まさに「My Favorites」だ。

　短編についての解説は「あとがき」に回すとして、ここではまず、英文を読むときの注意を書いておこう。

2. ヘミングウェイは難しい

　ヘミングウェイの作品は文が短く、簡潔だとよくいわれる。修飾語や修飾部をできるだけ省いた、客観描写の多い、ストレートな文体だともよくいわれる。きびきびした無駄のない文体だ。そんなスタイルをさして、「ハードボイルド」などと呼ぶ人も多い。「ハードボイルド」というのは料理の場合は、固ゆでの卵を指す。ぱさぱさの黄身のイメージからきているのかもしれない。

　だから読みやすい……と思っている人が多いが、そ

れは大間違いである。

　この注釈シリーズの4冊目で取り上げたサマセット・モームは長い文も多く、レトリカルで、ひねった表現も多く、また少し古い文体ということもあって、いまの若い人にはかなり読みづらいところもあったと思う。しかしヘミングウェイも負けず劣らず、読みづらい。

　たとえば、「キリマンジャロの雪」にしても冒頭の数行はあっけないほど読みやすいが、本文に入ると、あちこちで首をかしげてしまうはずだ。省略が多いうえに、It や That が何を指しているのかあいまいなところも頻出する。

　それ以外でも、たとえばこんなところは正直いって、よくわからない。

I'm getting as bored with dying as with everything else, he thought.
"It's a bore," he said out loud.
"What is, my dear?"
"Anything you do too bloody long." (68-70p)

　とくに最後の行。西崎憲の訳では「おまえがやることは何でもひどく時間がかかりすぎる」となっているし、高見浩訳では「おれは何をするんでも、時間をかけすぎるんだ」となっている。しかし、この 'you' は一般人称とも考えられるわけで、その場合は「人間ってのはなんだって、やるのがのろい（いつも手遅れ）」

となる。まあ、ヘミングウェイは翻訳家泣かせの作家でもあるのだ。

　さらにイタリック体になっているところ、つまり主人公のハリーがもうろうとした状態で過去を回想する部分は意味がとても取りづらい。このあたりは英語ネイティヴの人でもわかりづらいだろうし、おそらくよくわからないまま、あまり気にせずに読み飛ばすのだと思う。

　注はなるべくていねいに付けておいたが、細かく意味を取っていく必要はないだろう。

　「キリマンジャロの雪」とくらべると「フランシス・マカンバーの短く幸せな一生」のほうはまだましなほうだが、それでも読みやすいかときかれると、素直に「はい」とは答えられない。

　しかしそのぶん、日常感とリアリティ、緊迫感と切迫感、リズムとスピード感が生まれてくる。ヘミングウェイの文体の魅力はそんなところにあるのだろう。

　そんな文体を楽しんでみてほしい。

金原瑞人

contents

まえがき　金原瑞人 ········· 3

The Snows of Kilimanjaro ········· 9

The Short Happy Life of Francis Macomber ········· 81

あとがき　金原瑞人 ········· 177

装幀　眞島和馬

The Snows of Kilimanjaro

Kilimanjaro is a snow-covered mountain 19,710 feet high, and is said to be the highest mountain in Africa. Its western summit is called the Masai "Ngàje Ngài," the House of God. Close to the western summit there is the dried and frozen carcass of a leopard. No one has explained what the leopard was seeking at that altitude.

"The marvellous thing is that it's painless," he said. "That's how you know when it starts."

"Is it really?"

"Absolutely. I'm awfully sorry about the odor though. That must bother you."

"Don't! Please don't."

"Look at them," he said. "Now is it sight or is it scent that brings them like that?"

The cot the man lay on was in the wide shade of a mimosa tree and as he looked out past the shade onto the glare of the plain there were three of the big birds squatted obscenely, while in the sky a dozen more sailed, making quick-moving shadows as they passed.

"They've been there since the day the truck broke down," he said. "Today's the first time any have lit on the ground. I watched the way they sailed very carefully at first in case I ever wanted to use them in a story. That's funny now."

"I wish you wouldn't," she said.

"I'm only talking," he said. "It's much easier if I talk. But I don't want to bother you."

"You know it doesn't bother me," she said. "It's that

1 **feet** 1 foot は 30.48 cm 19,710 feet は 約 6,000m 3 **the Masai** マサイ族（ケニアの南部からタンザニアの北部に住んでいる部族） **Ngàje Ngài** マサイ語「神の館」 5 **carcass** 死骸 **leopard** ヒョウ 6 **altitude** 高度

8 **painless** 痛みのないこと 9 **That's how you know when it starts** 痛みがなくなると、それが始まったことがわかる（it が何かはそのうち明らかになる）

11 **awfully** とても **odor** 悪臭 13 **Don't!** やめてちょうだい！ 14 **them** 何を指しているかはそのうち明らかになる **is it sight or is it scent that brings them** やつらが集まってくるのは sight（死にかかっている獲物の姿）なのか、scent（におい）なのか

16 **cot** 簡易ベッド **mimosa** ミモザ 18 **glare of the plain** 太陽が照りつけている平原 **squatted** 翼をたたんでじっとしていた 19 **obscenely** いやらしい様子で

21 **broke down** 故障した 22 **any** =any big birds **have lit on the ground** 地面に降りてきた（lit は light の過去分詞） 24 **in case** 〜のときのために

26 **I wish you wouldn't** そんなことを言わないで

27 **It's much easier if I talk** しゃべっていると、とても楽なんだ

I've gotten so very nervous not being able to do anything. I think we might make it as easy as we can until the plane comes."

"Or until the plane doesn't come."

"Please tell me what I can do. There must be something I can do."

"You can take the leg off and that might stop it, though I doubt it. Or you can shoot me. You're a good shot now. I taught you to shoot, didn't I?"

"Please don't talk that way. Couldn't I read to you?"

"Read what?"

"Anything in the book bag that we haven't read."

"I can't listen to it," he said. "Talking is the easiest. We quarrel and that makes the time pass."

"I don't quarrel. I never want to quarrel. Let's not quarrel any more. No matter how nervous we get. Maybe they will be back with another truck today. Maybe the plane will come."

"I don't want to move," the man said. "There is no sense in moving now except to make it easier for you."

"That's cowardly."

"Can't you let a man die as comfortably as he can without calling him names? What's the use of slanging me?"

"You're not going to die."

"Don't be silly. I'm dying now. Ask those bastards." He looked over to where the huge, filthy birds sat, their naked heads sunk in the hunched feathers. A fourth planed down, to run quick-legged and then waddle

2 **we might make it as easy as we can**（この状態）を少しでもよくすることができるかもしれない
4 **until the plane doesn't come until the plane comes**「飛行機がくるまで」と言われたのに対して、「こない飛行機をいつまでも待っているあいだ」と皮肉をいっている
7 **take the leg off** この脚を切り落とす　**that might stop it** この状態に終止符を打つことができるかもしれない　9 **shot** 射撃手
10 **talk that way** そんなふうに言う　**Couldn't I read to you?** 何か読んであげましょうか？
14 **makes the time pass** 時間をつぶす
17 **they** あの人たち
19 **There is no sense** 意味がない　20 **make it easier for you** おまえの気が楽になる
21 **cowardly** 男らしくない
23 **calling him names** 相手の悪口を言う　**What's the use of slanging me?** おれを悪くいって、なんの得がある？　なにがおもしろい？
26 **ask those bastards** あいつらにきいてみろ　27 **filthy** ぞっとする、いまわしい　28 **hunched feathers** ふくらませた（翼の）羽根　**A fourth** 4羽目　29 **planed down** 舞いおりた　**quick-legged** 早足で　**waddle** よたよた歩いた

slowly toward the others.

"They are around every camp. You never notice them. You can't die if you don't give up."

"Where did you read that? You're such a bloody fool."

"You might think about some one else."

"For Christ's sake," he said, "that's been my trade."

He lay then and was quiet for a while and looked across the heat shimmer of the plain to the edge of the bush. There were a few Tommies that showed minute and white against the yellow and, far off, he saw a herd of zebra, white against the green of the bush. This was a pleasant camp under big trees against a hill, with good water, and close by, a nearly dry water hole where sand grouse flighted in the mornings.

"Wouldn't you like me to read?" she asked. She was sitting on a canvas chair beside his cot. "There's a breeze coming up."

"No thanks."

"Maybe the truck will come."

"I don't give a damn about the truck."

"I do."

"You give a damn about so many things that I don't."

"Not so many, Harry."

"What about a drink?"

"It's supposed to be bad for you. It said in Black's to avoid all alcohol. You shouldn't drink."

"Molo!" he shouted.

"Yes Bwana."

2 **They** ハゲワシ　**notice** 気がつく
4 **bloody fool** どうしようもないばか
7 **For Christ's sake** まったく、本当に　**my trade** 自分の仕事（作家業）
9 **heat shimmer** 熱気の揺れ　10 **Tommies** =Thomson's gazelle（トムソンガゼル）東アフリカによくいるガゼル　**minute** 小さい　11 **against** 〜を背景に　**a herd of zebra** シマウマの群
14 **water hole** 水たまり、小さな池　**sand grouse** 砂鶏（サケイ：ハトに似た鳥）　15 **flighted** （群れをなして）舞い降りてきた
17 **canvas chair** 座面と背もたれが帆布の椅子
21 **don't give a damn** どうでもいい
23 **give a damn** 気にする
24 **Harry** ハリー（主人公の名前）
25 **drink** 酒
26 **Black's** =Black's book ブラックという名前の医師の書いた本
28 **Molo** モーロ。いっしょに連れてきている現地の使用人の名前
29 **Bwana** ブワナ。スワヒリ語で男性に対する敬称。英語の sir とか master にあたる

"Bring whiskey-soda."

"Yes Bwana."

"You shouldn't," she said. "That's what I mean by giving up. It says it's bad for you. I know it's bad for you."

"No," he said. "It's good for me."

So now it was all over, he thought. So now he would never have a chance to finish it. So this was the way it ended, in a bickering over a drink. Since the gangrene started in his right leg he had no pain and with the pain the horror had gone and all he felt now was a great tiredness and anger that this was the end of it. For this, that now was coming, he had very little curiosity. For years it had obsessed him; but now it meant nothing in itself. It was strange how easy being tired enough made it.

Now he would never write the things that he had saved to write until he knew enough to write them well. Well, he would not have to fail at trying to write them either. Maybe you could never write them, and that was why you put them off and delayed the starting. Well he would never know, now.

"I wish we'd never come," the woman said. She was looking at him, holding the glass and biting her lip. "You never would have gotten anything like this in Paris. You always said you loved Paris. We could have stayed in Paris or gone anywhere. I'd have gone anywhere. I said I'd go anywhere you wanted. If you wanted to shoot we could have gone shooting in Hungary and been comfort-

₃ **That's what I mean by giving up** これは 14 ページ 3 行目の You can't die if you don't give up. を受けての科白。That は「酒を飲むこと」。つまり、「さっきわたしが『あきらめる』といったのは、お酒を飲むとか、そういうことよ」

₄ **It's says** It は前のページに出てきた Black's

₇ **So now it was all over** こうしてすべてが終わるのか ₈ **finish it** it は、彼が書こうとしていた本 **this was the way it ended** こうして終わるんだ ₉ **in a bickering over a drink** 酒のことで口論しているうちに **gangrene** 壊疽（えそ）。体の組織や細胞が死んでいくこと。10 ページ 9 行目の 'how you know when it starts' の it はこれのこと ₁₂ **tiredness** 疲労 **the end of it** こうして終わってしまう（死んでしまう）ということ **For this** このこと（死） ₁₃ **that now was coming** 今迫ってきている ₁₄ **it had obsessed** 死が取り憑いていた ₁₅ **being tired enough made it** 死に無関心になるほど疲れ切る

₁₈ **saved to write** 書くためにためてきた ₁₉ **not have to fail** （書こうとして）失敗することもない ₂₀ **you** 主人公、ハリーが自分のことを指して ₂₁ **put them off** 先延ばしにする **he would never know** 絶対にわからない

₂₃ **I wish we'd never come** （こんなところに）こなければよかった ₂₅ **never would have gotten anything like this** こんなことにならなくてすんだ ₂₇ **I'd** =I would ₂₈ **shoot** ハンティングをする

able."

"Your bloody money," he said.

"That's not fair," she said. "It was always yours as much as mine. I left everything and I went wherever you wanted to go and I've done what you wanted to do. But I wish we'd never come here."

"You said you loved it."

"I did when you were all right. But now I hate it. I don't see why that had to happen to your leg. What have we done to have that happen to us?"

"I suppose what I did was to forget to put iodine on it when I first scratched it. Then I didn't pay any attention to it because I never infect. Then, later, when it got bad, it was probably using that weak carbolic solution when the other antiseptics ran out that paralyzed the minute blood vessels and started the gangrene." He looked at her, "What else?"

"I don't mean that."

"If we would have hired a good mechanic instead of a half-baked Kikuyu driver, he would have checked the oil and never burned out that bearing in the truck."

"I don't mean that."

"If you hadn't left your own people, your goddamned Old Westbury, Saratoga, Palm Beach people to take me on ——"

"Why, I loved you. That's not fair. I love you now. I'll always love you. Don't you love me?"

"No," said the man. "I don't think so. I never have."

"Harry, what are you saying? You're out of your

2 **Your bloody money** おまえのいまいましい金
3 **That's not fair** そんな言い方ってないわ
4 **left everything** すべてを捨ててきた   6 **we'd** =we would（仮定法）
8 **when you were all right** あなたが健康だったときは
11 **iodine** ヨードチンキ（消毒殺菌剤）   12 **scratched it** it（右脚）にすり傷を作った   **Then** そのときは   13 **infect** 傷が化膿する   **Then** そして   14 **it was...that** it was that... の強調構文で、it と was と 15 行目の that を取ってみると構文がわかりやすい。'using that weak carbolic solution' が主語で、それを受ける動詞は 'paralyzed' と 'started'   **that weak carbolic solution** あの薄い石炭酸液   15 **antiseptics** 殺菌剤   **ran out** なかった   **paralyzed** 麻痺させた   **minute blood vessels** 毛細血管   17 **What else?** ほかに何が考えられる？
18 **I don't mean that** そんなことをいってるんじゃない
19 **mechanic** 整備工   20 **half-baked** 未熟な   **Kikuyu** キクユ族。主にケニアに住む部族   21 **bearing** 軸受け、ベアリング
23 **If you hadn't left your own people** もしおまえが親族のもとを離れなかったら   **goddamned** ろくでもない、いまいましい   24 **Old Westbury** オールド・ウェストベリ。ニューヨーク市郊外のナッソー郡にある村。州内でも最高級住宅地として有名   **Saratoga** サラトガ（ニューヨーク州の町）   **Palm Beach** パームビーチ（フロリダ州の東海岸にある避寒地）   **to take me on** おれを手に入れるために
26 **Why**（感嘆詞）「ああ、もう」
28 **I never have** =I never have loved you
29 **out of your head** 正気じゃない

head."

"No. I haven't any head to go out of."

"Don't drink that," she said. "Darling, please don't drink that. We have to do everything we can."

"You do it," he said. "I'm tired."

* * *

Now in his mind he saw a railway station at Karagatch and he was standing with his pack and that was the headlight of the Simplon-Orient cutting the dark now and he was leaving Thrace then after the retreat. That was one of the things he had saved to write, with, in the morning at breakfast, looking out the window and seeing snow on the mountains in Bulgaria and Nansen's Secretary asking the old man if it were snow and the old man looking at it and saying, No, that's not snow. It's too early for snow. And the Secretary repeating to the other girls, No, you see. It's not snow and them all saying, It's not snow we were mistaken. But it was the snow all right and he sent them on into it when he evolved exchange of populations. And it was snow they tramped along in until they died that winter.

It was snow too that fell all Christmas week that year up in the Gauertal, that year they lived in the woodcutter's house with the big square porcelain stove that filled half the room, and they slept on mattresses filled with beech leaves, the time the deserter came with his feet bloody in the snow. He said the police were right behind him and they gave him woolen socks and held the gendarmes talking until the tracks had drifted over.

2 **I haven't any head to go out of**（そもそも）正気を失うような頭を持っていない

7 **Karagatch** カラガッチ（トルコの地名） 9 **Simplon-Orient** シンプロン・オリエント急行 **cutting the dark** 闇を切り裂いて 10 **Thrace** トラキア（バルカン半島の東部） **the retreat**（軍隊の）退却 13 **Bulgaria** ブルガリア **Nansen's Secretary** ナンセン（ノルウェーの北極探検家・政治家。第1次世界大戦後の捕虜の送還、難民救済などで功績があった）の秘書 14 **the old man** ナンセンのこと 18 **It's not snow we were mistaken** あれは雪じゃなかった、わたしたちが間違っていた 19 **all right** やっぱり **into it** 雪の中へ **evolved exchange of populations**（ギリシアとトルコの）住民の交換移住を進展させた 20 **tramped** 踏みつけて歩いた

23 **up** 北の **the Gauertal** ガイエルタール（オーストリアの地名） 24 **big square porcelain stove** 大きくて四角い磁器のストーブ 26 **beech** ブナ **the time** そのとき **deserter** 脱走兵 27 **right behind** すぐ後ろに（right は強調） 28 **held the gendarmes talking** 話しかけて、警官たちを引き止めた 29 **until the tracks had drifted over** 足跡が雪でわからなくなるまで

In Schrunz, on Christmas day, the snow was so bright it hurt your eyes when you looked out from the Weinstube *and saw every one coming home from church. That was where they walked up the sleigh-smoothed urine-yellowed road along the river with the steep pine hills, skis heavy on the shoulder, and where they ran that great run down the glacier above the Madlenerhaus, the snow as smooth to see as cake frosting and as light as powder and he remembered the noiseless rush the speed made as you dropped down like a bird.*

They were snow-bound a week in the Madlener-haus that time in the blizzard playing cards in the smoke by the lantern light and the stakes were higher all the time as Herr Lent lost more. Finally he lost it all. Everything, the Skischule *money and all the season's profit and then his capital. He could see him with his long nose, picking up the cards and then opening, "Sans Voir." There was always gambling then. When there was no snow you gambled and when there was too much you gambled. He thought of all the time in his life he had spent gambling.*

But he had never written a line of that, nor of that cold, bright Christmas day with the mountains showing across the plain that Barker had flown across the lines to bomb the Austrian officers' leave train, machine-gunning them as they scattered and ran. He remembered Barker afterwards coming into the mess and starting to tell about it. And how quiet it got and then somebody saying, "You bloody murderous bastard."

Those were the same Austrians they killed then that

The Snows of Kilimanjaro

1 **Schrunz** シュルンス（Schruns。オーストリアの地名）
2 **Weinstube** ドイツやオーストリアのワイン酒場 4 **sleigh-smoothed** 橇でならされた 5 **urine-yellowed** 小便で黄色く染まった **pine** 松 7 **great run** 長い距離 **glacier** 氷河 **Madlener-haus** マドレーナーハウス（オーストリアの地名） 8 **as smooth to see as cake frosting** ケーキの糖衣のようになめらかに見える 9 **noiseless rush the speed made** スピードが作る無音の滑走

11 **snow-bound** 雪に閉じこめられた 12 **blizzard** 吹雪
13 **stakes** 賭けのレート 14 **as Herr Lent lost more** Herr は英語の Mr. にあたる。レント氏は負けるにつれて 15 **Skischule money** スキー学校で稼いだ金 **season's profit** その季節（冬）に稼いだ金 16 **capital** 元手 17 **Sans Voir** フランス語で、not seeing の意味。インディアン・ポーカーは、相手の札が見えて、自分の札が見えない状態でゲームをする 18 **then** そのとき
19 **when there was** snow が省略されている

23 **Barker** バーカー、味方の兵士 **lines** 戦闘の前線 24 **leave train** 休暇で国に帰る兵士を乗せた列車 26 **mess** 食堂
28 **murderous bastard** 人殺しの卑劣漢
29 **then** そのとき **that he skied with later** 後日、彼がいっしょにスキーをした

he skied with later. No not the same. Hans, that he skied with all that year, had been in the Kaiser-Jägers and when they went hunting hares together up the little valley above the saw-mill they had talked of the fighting on Pasubio and of the attack on Perticara and Asalone and he had never written a word of that. Nor of Monte Corona, nor the Sette Communi, nor of Arsiero.

How many winters had he lived in the Vorarlberg and the Arlberg? It was four and then he remembered the man who had the fox to sell when they had walked into Bludenz, that time to buy presents, and the cherry-pit taste of good kirsch, the fast-slipping rush of running powder-snow on crust, singing "Hi! Ho! said Rolly!" as you ran down the last stretch to the steep drop, taking it straight, then running the orchard in three turns and out across the ditch and onto the icy road behind the inn. Knocking your bindings loose, kicking the skis free and leaning them up against the wooden wall of the inn, the lamplight coming from the window, where inside, in the smoky, new-wine smelling warmth, they were playing the accordion.

"Where did we stay in Paris?" he asked the woman who was sitting by him in a canvas chair, now, in Africa.

"At the Crillon. You know that."

"Why do I know that?"

"That's where we always stayed."

"No. Not always."

"There and at the Pavillion Henri-Quatre in

2 **Kaiser-Jägers** ドイツ語で「チロルの山岳部隊」 3 **hares** 野ウサギ 4 **saw-mill** 製材所 5 **Pasubio** パスビオ（イタリアの地名） **Perticara and Asalone** ペルティカやアサローネ（両方ともイタリアの地名） 6 **Monte Corona** モンテ・コルノ。コルノ山（イタリアにある） 7 **Sette Communi** セッテ・コムーニ（イタリアの地名） **Arsiero** アルシエーロ（イタリアの地名）
8 **the Vorarlberg and the Arlberg** フォラルベルクやアルベルク（両方ともオーストリアの地名）。berg はドイツ語で「山」という意味なので the がついている 11 **Bludenz** ブルーデンツ（オーストリアの地名） **cherry-pit** サクランボの種 12 **taste of good kirsch** 上等なキルシュ（サクランボの果汁から作る蒸留酒） **fast-slipping rush of running powder-snow on crust** 凍った雪面を滑る粉雪のすごい速さ 13 **Hi! Ho! said Rolly** A Frog He Would A-Wooing というマザー・グースの歌の1節 14 **stretch** 距離 **steep drop** 急勾配の斜面 **taking it straight** 一直線に滑っていく 15 **in three turns** 3回のターンで 16 **ditch** 堀、溝 **inn** 宿屋、酒場 17 **Knocking your bindings loose** ビンディング（スキー板とブーツをつなぐ器具）をたたいてゆるめる **kicking the skis free** スキー板を蹴るようにしてはずす 18 **them** =the skis
25 **the Crillon** クリヨン（ホテルの名前）
29 **the Pavillion Henri-Quatre** パヴィヨン・アンリ・キャトル（ホテルの名前）

St. Germain. You said you loved it there."

"Love is a dunghill," said Harry. "And I'm the cock that gets on it to crow."

"If you have to go away," she said, "is it absolutely necessary to kill off everything you leave behind? I mean do you have to take away everything? Do you have to kill your horse, and your wife and burn your saddle and your armour?"

"Yes," he said. "Your damned money was my armour. My Swift and my Armour."

"Don't."

"All right. I'll stop that. I don't want to hurt you."

"It's a little bit late now."

"All right then. I'll go on hurting you. It's more amusing. The only thing I ever really liked to do with you I can't do now."

"No, that's not true. You liked to do many things and everything you wanted to do I did."

"Oh, for Christ sake stop bragging, will you?"

He looked at her and saw her crying.

"Listen," he said. "Do you think that it is fun to do this? I don't know why I'm doing it. It's trying to kill to keep yourself alive, I imagine. I was all right when we started talking. I didn't mean to start this, and now I'm crazy as a coot and being as cruel to you as I can be. Don't pay any attention, darling, to what I say. I love you, really. You know I love you. I've never loved any one else the way I love you."

He slipped into the familiar lie he made his bread and

The Snows of Kilimanjaro

1 **St.Germain** サンジェルマン（パリ西郊の都市）
2 **dunghill** 糞の山　**cock that gets on it to crow** その上に登って時をつくる雄鶏
5 **kill off** 全滅させる、すべてをだめにする　8 **saddle** 鞍　**armour** 鎧
10 **My Swift and my Armour** おれのスウィフトであり、おれのアーマー。スウィフトとアーマーは当時の有名なアメリカの富豪。armour と Armour をかけている。
11 **Don't** やめてよ
19 **for Christ sake** 頼むから　**bragging** 自慢する
21 **do this** こんなことをする　22 **It's trying to kill to keep yourself alive** yourself は一般人称だが、自分のことをいっている。自分を生かそうとするのは、(人を) 殺そうとすることだ
25 **coot** オオバンという鳥。coot はうるさい人間、頭のおかしい人間、無法者のたとえによく使われる　28 **the way I love you** おまえを愛するように
29 **slipped into** つい〜してしまった　**the familiar lie** いつもの嘘　**made his bread and butter by** それで収入を得ている

butter by.

"You're sweet to me."

"You bitch," he said. "You rich bitch. That's poetry. I'm full of poetry now. Rot and poetry. Rotten poetry."

"Stop it. Harry, why do you have to turn into a devil now?"

"I don't like to leave anything," the man said. "I don't like to leave things behind."

It was evening now and he had been asleep. The sun was gone behind the hill and there was a shadow all across the plain and the small animals were feeding close to camp; quick dropping heads and switching tails, he watched them keeping well out away from the bush now. The birds no longer waited on the ground. They were all perched heavily in a tree. There were many more of them. His personal boy was sitting by the bed.

"Memsahib's gone to shoot," the boy said. "Does Bwana want?"

"Nothing."

She had gone to kill a piece of meat and, knowing how he liked to watch the game, she had gone well away so she would not disturb this little pocket of the plain that he could see. She was always thoughtful, he thought. On anything she knew about, or had read, or that she had ever heard.

It was not her fault that when he went to her he was already over. How could a woman know that you meant nothing that you said; that you spoke only from habit

3 **bitch** 牝犬、いやな女　4 **I'm full of poetry** 詩的な気分でいっぱいだ　**Rot** たわごと　**Rotten poetry** どうしようもない詩
5 **turn into** 〜になる
13 **dropping heads** 頭を下げている　**switching tails** しっぽを振っている　14 **keeping well out away from** 〜から十分に離れている　16 **perched heavily** ずっしり重そうに（枝に）とまっている　17 **personal boy** 世話係の少年
18 **Memsahib's** Memsahib はスワヒリ語で女性に対する敬称。英語の lady にあたる　21 **kill a piece of meat** 食用の獲物を仕留める　22 **game** 獲物　**had gone well away** 十分に離れたところにいった　23 **disturb** 騒がせる　**this little pocket of the plain** この平原のポケットのようになっている場所　25 **On anything she knew about, or had read, or that she had ever heard** On は前の文の thoughtful につながっている。彼女は自分が知っていることや、読んだことや、聞いたことに関して thoughtful だということ
28 **over** （人間として）終わっている　**you meant nothing that you said** 自分のいったことはすべて本気ではなかった

and to be comfortable? After he no longer meant what he said, his lies were more successful with women than when he had told them the truth.

It was not so much that he lied as that there was no truth to tell. He had had his life and it was over and then he went on living it again with different people and more money, with the best of the same places, and some new ones.

You kept from thinking and it was all marvellous. You were equipped with good insides so that you did not go to pieces that way, the way most of them had, and you made an attitude that you cared nothing for the work you used to do, now that you could no longer do it. But, in yourself, you said that you would write about these people; about the very rich; that you were really not of them but a spy in their country; that you would leave it and write of it and for once it would be written by some one who knew what he was writing of. But he would never do it, because each day of not writing, of comfort, of being that which he despised, dulled his ability and softened his will to work so that, finally, he did no work at all. The people he knew now were all much more comfortable when he did not work. Africa was where he had been happiest in the good time of his life, so he had come out here to start again. They had made this safari with the minimum of comfort. There was no hardship; but there was no luxury and he had thought that he could get back into training that way. That in some way he could work the fat off his soul the way a fighter went

4 **It was not so much that he lied as that there was no truth to tell** 彼は嘘を並べたてたというよりは、語るべき真実がなかったのだ

9 **You** この段落の you は彼のこと　**kept from thinking** 考えることをやめていた　10 **equipped with good insides** 神経が太かった（inside は gut の意味）　**go to pieces** ぼろぼろになる　11 **the way most of them had** ほとんどの連中がそう（go to pieces）なるように　12 **you cared nothing for the work you used to do** 自分のしていた仕事なんかどうでもいい　13 **now that** いったん〜になると　15 **the very rich** 大金持　**not of them but a spy in their country** 彼らの一員ではなく、彼らの国にもぐりこんだスパイ　17 **for once** 初めて　20 **being that which** 自分が軽蔑しているもの　25 **They had made this safari with the minimum of comfort** ふたりはこのサファリ旅行をできるだけ簡素なものにした　28 **training** 鍛錬　**That** 前の文の he had thought を受けている　29 **work the fat off his soul** 自分の魂についた脂肪をそぎ落とす　**fighter** ボクサー

into the mountains to work and train in order to burn it out of his body.

She had liked it. She said she loved it. She loved anything that was exciting, that involved a change of scene, where there were new people and where things were pleasant. And he had felt the illusion of returning strength of will to work. Now if this was how it ended, and he knew it was, he must not turn like some snake biting itself because its back was broken. It wasn't this woman's fault. If it had not been she it would have been another. If he lived by a lie he should try to die by it. He heard a shot beyond the hill.

She shot very well this good, this rich bitch, this kindly caretaker and destroyer of his talent. Nonsense. He had destroyed his talent himself. Why should he blame this woman because she kept him well? He had destroyed his talent by not using it, by betrayals of himself and what he believed in, by drinking so much that he blunted the edge of his perceptions, by laziness, by sloth, and by snobbery, by pride and by prejudice, by hook and by crook. What was this? A catalogue of old books? What was his talent anyway? It was a talent all right but instead of using it, he had traded on it. It was never what he had done, but always what he could do. And he had chosen to make his living with something else instead of a pen or a pencil. It was strange, too, wasn't it, that when he fell in love with another woman, that woman should always have more money than the last one? But when he no longer was in love, when he

1 **burn it out of his body** それ（the fat）を体から燃焼させる 4 **involved a change of scene** 状況の変化もふくんだ 7 **if this was how it ended** もしこんなふうに終わるのなら 8 **he knew it was** こんなふうに終わることはわかっていたが **must not turn like some snake biting itself** 自分にかみつく蛇のように、後ろをふり向いてはならない 10 **If it had not been she** 彼女がいなかったとしても 11 **another** =another she 13 **shot very well** 射撃の腕がとてもよかった **this good, this rich bitch** このやさしくて、金持ちのいやな女 14 **caretaker** 世話役、世話人 16 **kept him well** やさしくしてくれた 19 **blunted the edge of his perceptions** 感覚、センスを鈍らせた 20 **sloth** 怠惰 **snobbery** 俗物根性 **by hook and by crook** あれやこれやで 23 **traded on it** それ（his talent）を使って商売をした **It was never what he had done, but always what he could do** それ（using it）を決して彼はしなかったが、（やろうと思えば）いつでもできたことだった 25 **make his living** 暮らしていく 28 **the last one** その前の女

was only lying, as to this woman, now, who had the most money of all, who had all the money there was, who had had a husband and children, who had taken lovers and been dissatisfied with them, and who loved him dearly as a writer, as a man, as a companion and as a proud possession; it was strange that when he did not love her at all and was lying, that he should be able to give her more for her money than when he had really loved.

We must all be cut out for what we do, he thought. However you make your living is where your talent lies. He had sold vitality, in one form or another, all his life and when your affections are not too involved you give much better value for the money. He had found that out but he would never write that, now, either. No, he would not write that, although it was well worth writing.

Now she came in sight, walking across the open toward the camp. She was wearing jodphurs and carrying her rifle. The two boys had a Tommie slung and they were coming along behind her. She was still a good-looking woman, he thought, and she had a pleasant body. She had a great talent and appreciation for the bed, she was not pretty, but he liked her face, she read enormously, liked to ride and shoot and, certainly, she drank too much. Her husband had died when she was still a comparatively young woman and for a while she had devoted herself to her two just-grown children, who did not need her and were embarrassed at having her about, to her stable of horses, to books, and to bottles.

The Snows of Kilimanjaro

1 **lying** 嘘をついていた　**as to this woman** この女に対してと同じように　2 **all the money there was** あるだけの金すべて　5 **dearly** 心から　6 **a proud possession** 虚栄心を満足させてくれる所有物　8 **for her money** 彼女のくれる金に対して

10 **We must all be cut out for what we do** おれたちは、自分のやることに合わせて作られているにちがいない　11 **However you make your living is where your talent lies** どうやって生計を立ていようが、そこにその人の才能がある　12 **vitality** 活力、命　**in one form or another** いろんな形で　13 **affections** 愛情　**involved** 夢中になっている

17 **open** 開けている場所、木などがない場所　18 **jodphurs** 膝下までのズボン、乗馬ズボン　19 **had a Tommie slung** ガゼルを肩に担いでいた　21 **pleasant** 魅力的な　22 **appreciation** 楽しむ才能　27 **had devoted herself** 専念した　**just-grown** 大人になったばかりの　28 **having her about** 彼女がそばにいる　29 **stable** 厩舎、馬屋　**bottles** 酒

She liked to read in the evening before dinner and she drank Scotch and soda while she read. By dinner she was fairly drunk and after a bottle of wine at dinner she was usually drunk enough to sleep.

That was before the lovers. After she had the lovers she did not drink so much because she did not have to be drunk to sleep. But the lovers bored her. She had been married to a man who had never bored her and these people bored her very much.

Then one of her two children was killed in a plane crash and after that was over she did not want the lovers, and drink being no anæsthetic she had to make another life. Suddenly, she had been acutely frightened of being alone. But she wanted some one that she respected with her.

It had begun very simply. She liked what he wrote and she had always envied the life he led. She thought he did exactly what he wanted to. The steps by which she had acquired him and the way in which she had finally fallen in love with him were all part of a regular progression in which she had built herself a new life and he had traded away what remained of his old life.

He had traded it for security, for comfort too, there was no denying that, and for what else? He did not know. She would have bought him anything he wanted. He knew that. She was a damned nice woman too. He would as soon be in bed with her as any one; rather with her, because she was richer, because she was very pleasant and appreciative and because she never made

3 **fairly** かなり
5 **before the lovers** 愛人が次々にできる前
11 **that was over** その事件が落ち着いた   12 **anæsthetic** 麻酔薬
20 **were** 主語は The steps と the way   **part of a regular progression** いつものお決まりの過程   22 **traded away** 売り渡した
23 **traded it for security** 身の保全（生きていくため）に売った **there was no denying that** それは否定しようがない
24 **He did not know** わからなかった   27 **would as soon be in bed with her as any one** ほかの女よりも彼女と寝たかった   **rather with her** 彼女のほうがいい   29 **appreciative** 積極的 **never made scenes** 男女関係のことで騒いだことがなかった

scenes. And now this life that she had built again was coming to a term because he had not used iodine two weeks ago when a thorn had scratched his knee as they moved forward trying to photograph a herd of waterbuck standing, their heads up, peering while their nostrils searched the air, their ears spread wide to hear the first noise that would send them rushing into the bush. They had bolted, too, before he got the picture.

Here she came now.

He turned his head on the cot to look toward her. "Hello," he said.

"I shot a Tommy ram," she told him. "He'll make you good broth and I'll have them mash some potatoes with the Klim. How do you feel?"

"Much better."

"Isn't that lovely? You know I thought perhaps you would. You were sleeping when I left."

"I had a good sleep. Did you walk far?"

"No. Just around behind the hill. I made quite a good shot on the Tommy."

"You shoot marvellously, you know."

"I love it. I've loved Africa. Really. If *you're* all right it's the most fun that I've ever had. You don't know the fun it's been to shoot with you. I've loved the country."

"I love it too."

"Darling, you don't know how marvellous it is to see you feeling better. I couldn't stand it when you felt that way. You won't talk to me like that again, will you? Promise me?"

2 **coming to a term** 終わろうとしていた　3 **thorn** 植物の刺　4 **herd** 群　**waterbuck** ウォーターバック（大型の羚羊）　5 **peering** 目を凝らす　**nostrils** 鼻孔　8 **bolted** 駆けだした
12 **Tommy ram** ガゼル　13 **broth** スープ　**have them mash some potatoes** ポーターたちにジャガイモをマッシュさせる
14 **Klim** 粉ミルク。商品名で milk を逆に綴っている
16 **lovely** うれしい
27 **stand** がまんする

"No," he said. "I don't remember what I said."

"You don't have to destroy me. Do you? I'm only a middle-aged woman who loves you and wants to do what you want to do. I've been destroyed two or three times already. You wouldn't want to destroy me again, would you?"

"I'd like to destroy you a few times in bed," he said.

"Yes. That's the good destruction. That's the way we're made to be destroyed. The plane will be here tomorrow."

"How do you know?"

"I'm sure. It's bound to come. The boys have the wood all ready and the grass to make the smudge. I went down and looked at it again today. There's plenty of room to land and we have the smudges ready at both ends."

"What makes you think it will come tomorrow?"

"I'm sure it will. It's overdue now. Then, in town, they will fix up your leg and then we will have some good destruction. Not that dreadful talking kind."

"Should we have a drink? The sun is down."

"Do you think you should?"

"I'm having one."

"We'll have one together. Molo, *letti dui* whiskey-soda!" she called.

"You'd better put on your mosquito boots," he told her.

"I'll wait till I bathe..."

While it grew dark they drank and just before it was

2 **destroy** ひどいめにあわせる

7 **destroy** いじめる、めちゃくちゃにする（セクシュアルな意味で）

8 **That's the way we're made to be destroyed** それこそわたしたちにふさわしい destroy され方

12 **It's bound to come** きっとくる　13 **smudge**（注意を引くための）煙、たき火　15 **room** 余裕

18 **overdue** 予定を過ぎている　20 **destruction** destroy すること　**Not that dreadful talking kind**（kind のあとに of destruction が省略されている）さっきみたいなひどい言い方をして destroy するんじゃなくて

24 **letti dui whiskey soda** ウイスキーソーダをふたつもってきて

26 **mosquito boots** 蚊よけのブーツ

dark and there was no longer enough light to shoot, a hyena crossed the open on his way around the hill.

"That bastard crosses there every night," the man said. "Every night for two weeks."

"He's the one makes the noise at night. I don't mind it. They're a filthy animal though."

Drinking together, with no pain now except the discomfort of lying in the one position, the boys lighting a fire, its shadow jumping on the tents, he could feel the return of acquiescence in this life of pleasant surrender. She *was* very good to him. He had been cruel and unjust in the afternoon. She was a fine woman, marvellous really. And just then it occurred to him that he was going to die.

It came with a rush; not as a rush of water nor of wind; but of a sudden evil-smelling emptiness and the odd thing was that the hyena slipped lightly along the edge of it.

"What is it, Harry?" she asked him.

"Nothing," he said. "You had better move over to the other side. To windward."

"Did Molo change the dressing?"

"Yes. I'm just using the boric now."

"How do you feel?"

"A little wobbly."

"I'm going in to bathe," she said. "I'll be right out. I'll eat with you and then we'll put the cot in."

So, he said to himself, we did well to stop the quarrelling. He had never quarrelled much with this woman,

2 **hyena** ハイエナ
6 **filthy** 不潔な、きたならしい
8 **in the one position** きまった格好で 10 **acquiescence** 大人しく受け入れる気持 **this life of pleasant surrender** この心地よい服従の人生 11 **unjust** 不当な、ひどい
15 **with a rush** いきなり 16 **evil-smelling emptiness** いやな臭いのする空虚感 17 **odd thing** 奇妙なこと **slipped lightly** 軽く駆けていった 18 **edge of it** it は a sudden evil-smelling emptiness
19 **What is it** どうしたの
21 **windward** 風上
22 **dressing** 包帯
23 **boric** ホウ酸
25 **wobbly** ふらふらする
26 **I'll be right out** すぐに出ていく 27 **put the cot in** その簡易ベッドを中に入れる

while with the women that he loved he had quarrelled so much they had finally, always, with the corrosion of the quarrelling, killed what they had together. He had loved too much, demanded too much, and he wore it all out.

He thought about alone in Constantinople that time, having quarrelled in Paris before he had gone out. He had whored the whole time and then, when that was over, and he had failed to kill his loneliness, but only made it worse, he had written her, the first one, the one who left him, a letter telling her how he had never been able to kill it. . . . How when he thought he saw her outside the Regence one time it made him go all faint and sick inside, and that he would follow a woman who looked like her in some way, along the Boulevard, afraid to see it was not she, afraid to lose the feeling it gave him. How every one he had slept with had only made him miss her more. How what she had done could never matter since he knew he could not cure himself of loving her. He wrote this letter at the Club, cold sober, and mailed it to New York asking her to write him at the office in Paris. That seemed safe. And that night missing her so much it made him feel hollow sick inside, he wandered up past Taxim's, picked a girl up and took her out to supper. He had gone to a place to dance with her afterward, she danced badly, and left her for a hot Armenian slut, that swung her belly against him so it almost scalded. He took her away from a British gunner

2 **the corrosion of the quarreling** けんかの腐食作用 3 **killed** だいなしにした 4 **wore it all out** 疲弊させた、すりへらした 7 **Constantinople** コンスタンチノープル（イスタンブールの旧称） 9 **whored** 売春婦を買った 11 **the first one** 最初の恋人 13 **How** どんなだったか（前の文の telling her を受けている） 14 **Regence** レジェンス（当時、パリのサントレノ通りにあったカフェ・ラ・レジェンスのこと） **made him go all faint and sick inside** 気を失いかけて、吐き気がした 16 **in some way** どことなく **the Boulevard** 大通り 18 **every one he had slept with had only made him miss her more** 彼はどんな女と寝ても、彼女をいっそう恋しく思うだけだった 20 **since** なぜなら **cure himself of loving her** 彼女を愛するという病を癒す 21 **the Club** 記者たちの出入りするクラブ（食事や酒が供される） **cold sober** 冷静で素面の状態 22 **the office in Paris** パリにあった支局 24 **hollow sick inside** 吐き気がするほど虚しい 25 **Taxim's** タクスィム広場 27 **left her for a hot Armenian slut** その女を捨てて、情熱的なアルメニアの売春婦と付き合った 28 **swung her belly against him** 腹を彼にすりつけてきた **so it almost scalded** 火傷になるほど 29 **took her away** 彼女を奪った **gunner subaltern** 砲兵隊の士官

subaltern after a row. The gunner asked him outside and they fought in the street on the cobbles in the dark. He'd hit him twice, hard, on the side of the jaw and when he didn't go down he knew he was in for a fight. The gunner hit him in the body, then beside his eye. He swung with his left again and landed and the gunner fell on him and grabbed his coat and tore the sleeve off and he clubbed him twice behind the ear and then smashed him with his right as he pushed him away. When the gunner went down his head hit first and he ran with the girl because they heard the M.P.'s coming. They got into a taxi and drove out to Rimmily Hissa along the Bosphorus, and around, and back in the cool night and went to bed and she felt as over-ripe as she looked but smooth, rose-petal, syrupy, smooth-bellied, big-breasted and needed no pillow under her buttocks, and he left her before she was awake looking blousy enough in the first daylight and turned up at the Pera Palace with a black eye, carrying his coat because one sleeve was missing.

That same night he left for Anatolia and he remembered, later on that trip, riding all day through fields of the poppies that they raised for opium and how strange it made you feel, finally, and all the distances seemed wrong, to where they had made the attack with the newly arrived Constantine officers, that did not know a goddamned thing, and the artillery had fired into the troops and the British observer had cried like a child.

That was the day he'd first seen dead men wearing white ballet skirts and upturned shoes with pompons on

1 row けんか 2 cobbles（道の）丸石 4 go down 倒れる was in for a fight かなり本気のけんかになりそうだ。be in for は「直面しそうな」という意味 5 swung with his left 左の拳でなぐった 6 landed 命中させた fell on 飛びかかった 8 clubbed なぐった 10 went down 倒れた his head hit first 頭を先に打った 11 **M.P.'s** M.P.=Military Police(man) 憲兵 12 Rimmily Hissa ルメリ・ヒサル。コンスタンティノープル郊外にある城塞 the Bosphorus ボスポラス海峡 14 as overripe as she looked 見た目通り、熟れすぎていた smooth, rose-petal, syrupy, smooth-bellied なめらかで、バラの花びらのようで、シロップのようで、なめらかな腹をしていた 16 buttocks 尻 17 blousy だらしない 18 turned up at ～に現れる Pera Palace ペラパラスホテル（1895年、イスタンブールにオープンした） black eye 目のまわりの青あざ 20 Anatolia アナトリア（黒海と地中海にはさまれた高原部分。小アジアのこと） 21 fields of the poppies ケシ畑 22 raised for opium 阿片を作るために育てられていた 23 all the distances seemed wrong 距離感がつかめなくなった 24 the newly arrived Constantine officers 新たにやってきたコンスタンティノス王の将校たち 25 did not know a goddamned thing 本当に何も知らない 26 artillery 大砲 troops 軍隊 27 observer 観戦武官
29 ballet skirts バレエの白いスカート upturned shoes 先が上を向いている靴 pompons 房飾り

them. The Turks had come steadily and lumpily and he had seen the skirted men running and the officers shooting into them and running then themselves and he and the British observer had run too until his lungs ached and his mouth was full of the taste of pennies and they stopped behind some rocks and there were the Turks coming as lumpily as ever. Later he had seen the things that he could never think of and later still he had seen much worse. So when he got back to Paris that time he could not talk about it or stand to have it mentioned. And there in the café as he passed was that American poet with a pile of saucers in front of him and a stupid look on his potato face talking about the Dada movement with a Roumanian who said his name was Tristan Tzara, who always wore a monocle and had a headache, and, back at the apartment with his wife that now he loved again, the quarrel all over, the madness all over, glad to be home, the office sent his mail up to the flat. So then the letter in answer to the one he'd written came in on a platter one morning and when he saw the handwriting he went cold all over and tried to slip the letter underneath another. But his wife said, "Who is that letter from, dear?" and that was the end of the beginning of that.

He remembered the good times with them all, and the quarrels. They always picked the finest places to have the quarrels. And why had they always quarrelled when he was feeling best? He had never written any of that because, at first, he never wanted to hurt any one

The Snows of Kilimanjaro

1 **Turks** トルコ軍　**lumpily** 重い足音を響かせて　2 **skirted men** スカートをはいた兵士たち　5 **taste of pennies** 銅貨の味（pennyは1セント銅貨）　7 **the things that he could never think of** 彼が思いもよらなかった（ほど酷い）もの　10 **stand** 耐える　**have it mentioned** そのことが口にされる　11 **there in the café as he passed was that American poet** 彼が通りかかったカフェにアメリカ人の詩人がいた　12 **a pile of saucers** 積みあげた皿　**a stupid look on his potato face** ジャガイモのような顔に間抜けな表情を浮かべた　13 **Dada movement** ダダ運動（20世紀初め、第1次世界大戦を機に起こった文芸・芸術運動。シュールリアリスムにつながっていく）　14 **Roumanian** ルーマニア人　**Tristan Tzara** トリスタン・ツァラ（ダダ運動の中心的人物）　15 **monocle** 片眼鏡　17 **all over** 終わった　19 **flat** アパート　20 **on a platter** ゆうゆうと、堂々と　21 **all over** 全身　22 **another** =another letter　23 **the beginning of that** 新しく始まったこと（妻のもとにもどっての生活）　25 **them** 付き合ってきた女たち

and then it seemed as though there was enough to write without it. But he had always thought that he would write it finally. There was so much to write. He had seen the world change; not just the events; although he had seen many of them and had watched the people, but he had seen the subtler change and he could remember how the people were at different times. He had been in it and he had watched it and it was his duty to write of it; but now he never would.

"How do you feel?" she said. She had come out from the tent now after her bath.

"All right."

"Could you eat now?" He saw Molo behind her with the folding table and the other boy with the dishes.

"I want to write," he said.

"You ought to take some broth to keep your strength up."

"I'm going to die tonight," he said. "I don't need my strength up."

"Don't be melodramatic, Harry, please," she said.

"Why don't you use your nose? I'm rotted half way up my thigh now. What the hell should I fool with broth for? Molo bring whiskey-soda."

"Please take the broth," she said gently.

"All right."

The broth was too hot. He had to hold it in the cup until it cooled enough to take it and then he just got it down without gagging.

₃ **finally** そのうちきっと　₄ **not just the events** 起こったことだけではなく　₆ **subtler** もっと微妙な　₇ **at different times** 違うときには　**it** そのときの状況
₁₇ **keep your strength up** 体力をつける
₂₂ **I'm rotted** 自分はもう腐っている　**half way up my thigh** 太腿の半分くらいまで　₂₃ **the hell** まったく（強調）　**fool with broth** スープでごまかす
₂₉ **gagging** 喉に詰まらせる

"You're a fine woman," he said. "Don't pay any attention to me."

She looked at him with her well-known, well-loved face from *Spur* and *Town and Country,* only a little the worse for drink, only a little the worse for bed, but *Town and Country* never showed those good breasts and those useful thighs and those lightly small-of-back-caressing hands, and as he looked and saw her well-known pleasant smile, he felt death come again. This time there was no rush. It was a puff, as of a wind that makes a candle flicker and the flame go tall.

"They can bring my net out later and hang it from the tree and build the fire up. I'm not going in the tent tonight. It's not worth moving. It's a clear night. There won't be any rain."

So this was how you died, in whispers that you did not hear. Well, there would be no more quarrelling. He could promise that. The one experience that he had never had he was not going to spoil now. He probably would. You spoiled everything. But perhaps he wouldn't.

"You can't take dictation, can you?"

"I never learned," she told him.

"That's all right."

There wasn't time, of course, although it seemed as though it telescoped so that you might put it all into one paragraph if you could get it right.

There was a log house, chinked white with mortar, on

3 **well-known** 多くの人に知られた　**well-loved** 多くの人に愛された　4 **Spur** 雑誌の名　**Town and Country** 雑誌の名前　**only little the worse for drink** 飲酒のせいでそのぶん少し容色が衰えて（the は副詞で、「それだけ、そのぶんだけ」の意味）　5 **bed** セックス　6 **showed** 本や雑誌に掲載された　7 **small-of-back-caressing** 腰をなでる　10 **puff** 軽い息　**as of** ～のような　11 **flicker** ゆらめく　**go tall** 大きくなる

12 **net** 蚊帳　13 **build the fire up** 火をおこす　14 **It's not worth moving** わざわざ移動することはない

16 **this was how you died** こうやって死んでいくんだな　**in whispers** ささやき声のなかで　18 **The one experience that he had never had** 彼が今までしなかった唯一の経験（これはこのあとの spoil の目的語になっている）　19 **spoil** だいなしにする　**He probably would** このあとに spoil が省略されている　20 **You** 主人公が自分にむかっていっている

22 **take dictation** 相手が語ったことを書きとる

26 **telescoped** 短縮する　**put it all into one paragraph** 1段落にしてしまう　27 **get it right** うまくやる

29 **log house** ログハウス、丸太小屋　**chinked** すき間をふさいだ　**mortar** モルタル

a hill above the lake. There was a bell on a pole by the door to call the people in to meals. Behind the house were fields and behind the fields was the timber. A line of lombardy poplars ran from the house to the dock. Other poplars ran along the point. A road went up to the hills along the edge of the timber and along that road he picked blackberries. Then that log house was burned down and all the guns that had been on deer foot racks above the open fire place were burned and afterwards their barrels, with the lead melted in the magazines, and the stocks burned away, lay out on the heap of ashes that were used to make lye for the big iron soap kettles, and you asked Grandfather if you could have them to play with, and he said, no. You see they were his guns still and he never bought any others. Nor did he hunt any more. The house was rebuilt in the same place out of lumber now and painted white and from its porch you saw the poplars and the lake beyond; but there were never any more guns. The barrels of the guns that had hung on the deer feet on the wall of the log house lay out there on the heap of ashes and no one ever touched them.

In the Black Forest, after the war, we rented a trout stream and there were two ways to walk to it. One was down the valley from Triberg and around the valley road in the shade of the trees that bordered the white road, and then up a side road that went up through the hills past many small farms, with the big Schwarzwald *houses, until that road crossed the stream. That was*

3 **timber** 林、森 4 **lombardy poplars** セイヨウハコヤナギ **dock** 波止場 5 **point** 海岸の突端、岬 7 **blackberries** クロイチゴ **burned down** 火事で燃えてしまった 8 **deer foot racks** シカの足を使って作った銃の棚 9 **open fire place** 暖炉の上 10 **barrels** 銃身 **lead** 鉛、銃弾 **magazines** 弾倉 11 **stocks** 銃床（銃器の銃身を支える木製の部分） 12 **lye** 灰汁（木の灰を水にまぜてこし取ったもの） **iron soap kettles** 石鹸を作る鉄鍋 16 **out of lumber**（丸太ではなく）板で
23 **the Black Forest**「黒い森」。ドイツ語ではSchwarzwald。ドイツ南西部の森林地帯（『武器よさらば』にも出てくる） **trout stream** マスのいる川 25 **Triberg** トリベルク（「黒い森」にある町の名前）

where our fishing began.

The other way was to climb steeply up to the edge of the woods and then go across the top of the hills through the pine woods, and then out to the edge of a meadow and down across this meadow to the bridge. There were birches along the stream and it was not big, but narrow, clear and fast, with pools where it had cut under the roots of the birches. At the Hotel in Triberg the proprietor had a fine season. It was very pleasant and we were all great friends. The next year came the inflation and the money he had made the year before was not enough to buy supplies to open the hotel and he hanged himself.

You could dictate that, but you could not dictate the Place Contrescarpe where the flower sellers dyed their flowers in the street and the dye ran over the paving where the autobus started and the old men and the women, always drunk on wine and bad marc; and the children with their noses running in the cold; the smell of dirty sweat and poverty and drunkenness at the Café des Amateurs and the whores at the Bal Musette they lived above. The concierge who entertained the trooper of the Garde Republicaine in her loge, his horse-hair-plumed helmet on a chair. The locataire across the hall whose husband was a bicycle racer and her joy that morning at the crémerie *when she had opened* L'Auto *and seen where he placed third in Paris-Tours, his first big race. She had blushed and laughed and then gone upstairs crying with the yellow sporting paper in her hand. The husband of the woman who ran the Bal Musette drove a*

The Snows of Kilimanjaro

4 **meadow** 牧草地、草地 6 **birches** カバの木 7 **pools** 深み
8 **proprietor** 経営者 9 **had a fine season** 経営状態がよかった
12 **supplies** 備品や食料品
13 **You could dictate that**（その気になれば）ここまでの部分（52ページの最後の行から56ページの12行目まで）は、自分で語ってそれを書き留めてもらうことができる 14 **Place Contrescarpe** コントレスカルプ広場（パリにある） **dyed** 染めた 15 **the dye** 染料 **ran over the paving** 舗道の上を流れていた 17 **marc** マークブランデー（安酒） 18 **with their noses running** はなをたらして 19 **the Café des Amateurs** カフェ・デザマトゥール 20 **whores** 娼婦たち **the Bal Musette** バル・ミュゼット（大衆的なダンスホール） 21 **concierge** 門番、玄関番 **the trooper of the Garde Republicaine** パリ憲兵隊（パリ市内の警備を務める一方、儀仗兵も務める） 22 **loge** 小部屋、個室 **his horse-hair-plumed helmet** 馬の毛の飾りのついたヘルメット 23 **locataire** 借家人 25 **crémerie** 簡易食堂 **L'Auto** 自動車 26 **placed third** 三位になった **Paris-Tours** パリ・トゥール（フランス西部の街）間 27 **blushed** 顔を赤くした
28 **sporting paper** スポーツ新聞 29 **ran** 経営していた

taxi and when he, Harry, had to take an early plane the husband knocked upon the door to wake him and they each drank a glass of white wine at the zinc of the bar before they started. He knew his neighbors in that quarter then because they all were poor.

Around that Place there were two kinds; the drunkards and the sportifs. *The drunkards killed their poverty that way; the* sportifs *took it out in exercise. They were the descendants of the Communards and it was no struggle for them to know their politics. They knew who had shot their fathers, their relatives, their brothers, and their friends when the Versailles troops came in and took the town after the Commune and executed any one they could catch with calloused hands, or who wore a cap, or carried any other sign he was a working man. And in that poverty, and in that quarter across the street from a Boucherie Chevaline and a wine co-operative he had written the start of all he was to do. There never was another part of Paris that he loved like that, the sprawling trees, the old white plastered houses painted brown below, the long green of the autobus in that round square, the purple flower dye upon the paving, the sudden drop down the hill of the rue Cardinal Lemoine to the River, and the other way the narrow crowded world of the rue Mouffetard. The street that ran up toward the Pantheon and the other that he always took with the bicycle, the only asphalted street in all that quarter, smooth under the tires, with the high narrow houses and the cheap tall hotel where Paul Verlaine had died. There*

The Snows of Kilimanjaro

3 **zinc** 亜鉛でメッキしたカウンター
6 **drunkards** 飲んだくれ 7 **sportifs** スポーツ好き 8 **that way** そうやって、酒を飲んで **took it out** it（poverty）を取りのぞく 9 **descendants** 子孫 **Communards** パリコミューン（1871年、パリ市民、労働者が蜂起して樹立した社会主義的革命政権。72日間で崩壊）の支持者 10 **struggle** 苦悩 12 **the Versailles troops** ヴェルサイユの兵士たち（政府軍） 13 **after the Commune** コミューンが崩壊してから **executed** 処刑した 14 **calloused hands** たこができた手（労働者の手） **wore a cap** キャップをかぶっていた（当時の労働者はよくキャップをかぶっていた） 16 **quarter** 地区 17 **Boucherie Chevaline** 馬肉を扱う肉屋 **wine co-operative** ワイン協同組合 20 **sprawling** 不規則に枝が広がる **plastered** 漆喰を塗った 21 **autobus** バス **round square** 円形広場 23 **the rue Cardinal Lemoine** カルディナル・ルモワーヌ通り（rue は「通り」） 24 **the River** セーヌ川 **the other way** 反対側 25 **the rue Mouffetard** ムフタール通り 26 **the Pantheon** パンテオン（18世紀に教会として建てられた。現在は、フランスの身分の高い人や、キュリー夫妻、ユゴー、モネなど、功績のあった人が埋葬されている） **took with the bicycle** 自転車で走った 29 **Paul Verlaine** ポール・ヴェルレーヌ（フランスの詩人）

were only two rooms in the apartments where they lived and he had a room on the top floor of that hotel that cost him sixty francs a month where he did his writing, and from it he could see the roofs and chimney pots and all the hills of Paris.

From the apartment you could only see the wood and coal man's place. He sold wine too, bad wine. The golden horse's head outside the Boucherie Chevaline where the carcasses hung yellow gold and red in the open window, and the green painted co-operative where they bought their wine; good wine and cheap. The rest was plaster walls and the windows of the neighbors. The neighbors who, at night, when some one lay drunk in the street, moaning and groaning in that typical French ivresse *that you were propaganded to believe did not exist, would open their windows and then the murmur of talk.*

"Where is the policeman? When you don't want him the bugger is always there. He's sleeping with some concierge. Get the Agent." Till some one threw a bucket of water from a window and the moaning stopped. "What's that? Water. Ah, that's intelligent." And the windows shutting. Marie, his femme de ménage, *protesting against the eight-hour day saying, "If a husband works until six he gets only a little drunk on the way home and does not waste too much. If he works only until five he is drunk every night and one has no money. It is the wife of the working man who suffers from this shortening of hours."*

3 **francs** フラン。当時のフランスの通貨 4 **chimney pots** 煙突の先に付けてある通風管

7 **coal man's place** 石炭を売っている店 **golden horse's head** 金色の馬の頭（看板） 9 **the carcasses hung** 切り分けた馬の部位が下がっていた **yellow gold and red** 金色っぽい黄色と赤の 14 **moaning** うめきながら **groaning** うなりながら 15 **ivresse** フランス語で「酔っぱらっている状態」 **propaganded to believe** 〜と信じる（考える）ようにと宣伝されていた **did not exist** 存在しない 16 **murmur of talk** ほそぼそとしゃべること

19 **bugger** 野郎 20 **Get the Agent** 警官を連れてこい 22 **intelligent** 頭がいい（上から水をかけたことに対して） 23 **femme de ménage** フランス語で「家政婦」 24 **eight-hour day** 1日8時間制

"Wouldn't you like some more broth?" the woman asked him now.

"No, thank you very much. It is awfully good."

"Try just a little."

"I would like a whiskey-soda."

"It's not good for you."

"No. It's bad for me. Cole Porter wrote the words and the music. This knowledge that you're going mad for me."

"You know I like you to drink."

"Oh yes. Only it's bad for me."

When she goes, he thought, I'll have all I want. Not all I want but all there is. Ayee he was tired. Too tired. He was going to sleep a little while. He lay still and death was not there. It must have gone around another street. It went in pairs, on bicycles, and moved absolutely silently on the pavements.

No, he had never written about Paris. Not the Paris that he cared about. But what about the rest that he had never written?

What about the ranch and the silvered gray of the sage brush, the quick, clear water in the irrigation ditches, and the heavy green of the alfalfa. The trail went up into the hills and the cattle in the summer were shy as deer. The bawling and the steady noise and slow moving mass raising a dust as you brought them down in the fall. And behind the mountains, the clear sharp-

4 **awfully good** とてもおいしい
8 **Cole Porter** コール・ポーター（1893 – 1964。アメリカの作曲家） **wrote the words and the music** 歌詞も曲も作った。彼の有名な曲に 'It's bad for Me' というのがあり、そのなかに 'it's bad for me, this knowledge that you're going mad for me' （ぼくは困ってしまう、君がぼくに夢中だとわかっちゃうと）という1節がある。
13 **Not all I want but all there is** 飲みたいだけ飲むんじゃなくて、ありったけ全部飲む　14 **Ayee he was tired** あーあ、まったく疲れちまった（主人公の心の中のぼやき）　16 **It** =death
17 **in pairs** ふたり組で（連れていく人間といっしょに）
20 **Not the Paris that he cared about** 自分の好きだったパリについては書かなかった　21 **rest** 残り。パリの話以外のこと
23 **ranch** 牧場　24 **sage brush** セージの畑　**irrigation ditches** 灌漑用の溝　25 **alfalfa** ムラサキウマゴヤシ（牧草）　**trail** 小道　26 **cattle** 牛　27 **bawling** 大きな声　**steady noise** ひっきりなしにたてる音　28 **mass** （牛の）群

ness of the peak in the evening light and, riding down along the trail in the moonlight, bright across the valley. Now he remembered coming down through the timber in the dark holding the horse's tail when you could not see and all the stories that he meant to write.

About the half-wit chore boy who was left at the ranch that time and told not to let any one get any hay, and that old bastard from the Forks who had beaten the boy when he had worked for him stopping to get some feed. The boy refusing and the old man saying he would beat him again. The boy got the rifle from the kitchen and shot him when he tried to come into the barn and when they came back to the ranch he'd been dead a week, frozen in the corral, and the dogs had eaten part of him. But what was left you packed on a sled wrapped in a blanket and roped on and you got the boy to help you haul it, and the two of you took it out over the road on skis, and sixty miles down to town to turn the boy over. He having no idea that he would be arrested. Thinking he had done his duty and that you were his friend and he would be rewarded. He'd helped to haul the old man in so everybody could know how bad the old man had been and how he'd tried to steal some feed that didn't belong to him, and when the sheriff put the handcuffs on the boy he couldn't believe it. Then he'd started to cry. That was one story he had saved to write. He knew at least twenty good stories from out there and he had never written one. Why?

1 **riding along the trail** 小道を馬で駆け下りる 3 **timber** 林、森 5 **meant to write** 書くつもりだった
6 **half-wit** 頭の鈍い、知恵の足りない **chore boy** 雑用をやっていた少年 7 **get any hay** 干し草を取っていく 8 **that old bastard** あの老いぼれ **the Forks** フォークス家 9 **get some feed** 餌（干し草）を取っていく 12 **barn** 納屋 13 **he'd been dead a week** 死んで一週間たっていた 14 **corral** 畜舎 15 **what was left** 死骸の残った部分 **sled** 橇 17 **haul** 引っぱる 18 **turn the boy over** その少年を引き渡す 21 **rewarded** 礼をもらう 24 **sheriff** 保安官 **handcuffs** 手錠 26 **saved to write** 書くために取ってあった 27 **out there** あそこ、牧場やそのまわり

"You tell them why," he said.
"Why what, dear?"
"Why nothing."

She didn't drink so much, now, since she had him. But if he lived he would never write about her, he knew that now. Nor about any of them. The rich were dull and they drank too much, or they played too much backgammon. They were dull and they were repetitious. He remembered poor Julian and his romantic awe of them and how he had started a story once that began, "The very rich are different from you and me." And how some one had said to Julian, Yes, they have more money. But that was not humorous to Julian. He thought they were a special glamourous race and when he found they weren't it wrecked him just as much as any other thing that wrecked him.

He had been contemptuous of those who wrecked. You did not have to like it because you understood it. He could beat anything, he thought, because no thing could hurt him if he did not care.

All right. Now he would not care for death. One thing he had always dreaded was the pain. He could stand pain as well as any man, until it went on too long, and wore him out, but here he had something that had hurt frightfully and just when he had felt it breaking him, the pain had stopped.

He remembered long ago when Williamson, the bombing officer, had been hit by a stick bomb some one

1 **You tell them why** 連中に、なぜだか教えてやれ（命令形）
2 **Why what** なぜって、なんのこと
3 **Why nothing** なぜ、どうしようもないかってことを
4 **she had him** 彼女は彼を手に入れた   5 **if he lived** もし生きながらえたとしても   6 **dull** 退屈   7 **backgammon** バックギャモン   8 **repetitious** 同じことを繰り返してばかりいる   9 **romantic awe of them** 彼ら（金持ち）に対するロマンチックな尊敬   13 **that was not humorous to Julian**（相手は冗談のつもりでいったのに）ジュリアンには冗談とは思えなかった   14 **glamourous race** とびぬけて魅力的な人種   15 **wrecked** たたきつぶした

17 **contemptuous** 軽蔑的な   **wrecked** たたきつぶされた
18 **You did not have to like it because you understood it** 理解できるからといって、好きになる必要はない   19 **beat** 打ちのめす   20 **care** 気にする、気にかける
24 **wore him out** 消耗させた   25 **frightfully** ぞっとするほど
29 **bombing officer** 爆撃班の士官   **stick bomb** 手榴弾

in a German patrol had thrown as he was coming in through the wire that night and, screaming, had begged every one to kill him. He was a fat man, very brave, and a good officer, although addicted to fantastic shows. But that night he was caught in the wire, with a flare lighting him up and his bowels spilled out into the wire, so when they brought him in, alive, they had to cut him loose. Shoot me, Harry. For Christ sake shoot me. They had had an argument one time about our Lord never sending you anything you could not bear and some one's theory had been that meant that at a certain time the pain passed you out automatically. But he had always remembered Williamson, that night. Nothing passed out Williamson until he gave him all his morphine tablets that he had always saved to use himself and then they did not work right away.

Still this now, that he had, was very easy; and if it was no worse as it went on there was nothing to worry about. Except that he would rather be in better company.

He thought a little about the company that he would like to have.

No, he thought, when everything you do, you do too long, and do too late, you can't expect to find the people still there. The people all are gone. The party's over and you are with your hostess now.

I'm getting as bored with dying as with everything else, he thought.

"It's a bore," he said out loud.

1 **patrol** 偵察隊、哨戒隊　**in through the wire** 鉄条網をくぐって　4 **addicted** 〜に中毒になっていた　**fantastic shows** オーバーなジェスチャーをすること、大げさに見せること　5 **flare** 照明弾（空中で炸裂して、強烈な光を発する）　6 **bowels** 腸　7 **cut him loose** 腸を切って彼を鉄条網から引き離す　8 **For Christ sake** 頼むから　9 **Lord** 主、神　10 **bear** 耐える　12 **passed you out** 気を失わせる　14 **morphine tablets** モルヒネ（鎮痛剤）の錠剤　16 **right away** すぐに

18 **Still** しかし　**that he had** 彼が抱えていた苦痛　19 **it went on** この状態が続く　20 **would rather** できれば〜したい　**in better company** もっといい相手

27 **as bored with dying as with everything else** ほかのことと同様、死ぬことにも飽きている

"What is, my dear?"

"Anything you do too bloody long."

He looked at her face between him and the fire. She was leaning back in the chair and the firelight shone on her pleasantly lined face and he could see that she was sleepy. He heard the hyena make a noise just outside the range of the fire.

"I've been writing," he said. "But I got tired."

"Do you think you will be able to sleep?"

"Pretty sure. Why don't you turn in?"

"I like to sit here with you."

"Do you feel anything strange?" he asked her.

"No. Just a little sleepy."

"I do," he said.

He had just felt death come by again.

"You know the only thing I've never lost is curiosity," he said to her.

"You've never lost anything. You're the most complete man I've ever known."

"Christ," he said. "How little a woman knows. What is that? Your intuition?"

Because, just then, death had come and rested its head on the foot of the cot and he could smell its breath.

"Never believe any of that about a scythe and a skull," he told her. "It can be two bicycle policemen as easily, or be a bird. Or it can have a wide snout like a hyena."

It had moved up on him now, but it had no shape any more. It simply occupied space.

2 **Anything you do too bloody long** 人のやることはなんでものろい（you は一般人称）
4 **was leaning back in the chair** 椅子の背にもたれかかっていた　5 **lined** 皺のある　7 **range of the fire** 火の光が届く範囲
10 **Pretty** とても　**turn in** 床に就く、寝る
20 **Christ** まったく　21 **intuition** 直感
23 **the foot of the cot** 簡易ベッドの足側（寝て、足を置く方）
24 **scythe** 大鎌　25 **skull** 頭蓋骨（大鎌も頭蓋骨も死神の象徴）
It can be two bicycle policemen それは自転車に乗ったふたりの警官になるかもしれない　**as easily** 簡単に　26 **snout** 鼻面（このあたり、しゃべることが支離滅裂になってきている）

"Tell it to go away."

It did not go away but moved a little closer.

"You've got a hell of a breath," he told it. "You stinking bastard."

It moved up closer to him still and now he could not speak to it, and when it saw he could not speak it came a little closer, and now he tried to send it away without speaking, but it moved in on him so its weight was all upon his chest, and while it crouched there and he could not move, or speak, he heard the woman say, "Bwana is asleep now. Take the cot up very gently and carry it into the tent."

He could not speak to tell her to make it go away and it crouched now, heavier, so he could not breathe. And then, while they lifted the cot, suddenly it was all right and the weight went from his chest.

It was morning and had been morning for some time and he heard the plane. It showed very tiny and then made a wide circle and the boys ran out and lit the fires, using kerosene, and piled on grass so there were two big smudges at each end of the level place and the morning breeze blew them toward the camp and the plane circled twice more, low this time, and then glided down and levelled off and landed smoothly and, coming walking toward him, was old Compton in slacks, a tweed jacket and a brown felt hat.

"What's the matter, old cock?" Compton said.

"Bad leg," he told him. "Will you have some break-

The Snows of Kilimanjaro

3 **a hell of a breath** ひどく息の臭い　**stinking** 悪臭を放つ
7 **send it away** 追いやる
9 **crouched** うずくまっていた
21 **kerosene** 灯油　**piled on grass** 草を積んだ　22 **smudges** 煙、たき火　**level place** 平らな場所　25 **levelled off**（機体を）水平にした　26 **tweed** ツイード　27 **felt hat** フェルトの帽子
28 **old cock** 男に対する親しい呼びかけ

fast?"

"Thanks. I'll just have some tea. It's the Puss Moth you know. I won't be able to take the Memsahib. There's only room for one. Your lorry is on the way."

Helen had taken Compton aside and was speaking to him. Compton came back more cheery than ever.

"We'll get you right in," he said. "I'll be back for the Mem. Now I'm afraid I'll have to stop at Arusha to refuel. We'd better get going."

"What about the tea?"

"I don't really care about it, you know."

The boys had picked up the cot and carried it around the green tents and down along the rock and out onto the plain and along past the smudges that were burning brightly now, the grass all consumed, and the wind fanning the fire, to the little plane. It was difficult getting him in, but once in he lay back in the leather seat, and the leg was stuck straight out to one side of the seat where Compton sat. Compton started the motor and got in. He waved to Helen and to the boys and, as the clatter moved into the old familiar roar, they swung around with Compie watching for wart-hog holes and roared, bumping, along the stretch between the fires and with the last bump rose and he saw them all standing below, waving, and the camp beside the hill, flattening now, and the plain spreading, clumps of trees, and the bush flattening, while the game trails ran now smoothly to the dry waterholes, and there was a new water that he had never known of. The zebra, small rounded backs now,

2 **the Puss Moth** プス・モス。小型の自家用機　4 **lorry** トラック
5 **taken Compton aside** コンプトンをわきに連れていった
7 **get you right in** 君をすぐに乗せる　8 **Mem** =Memsahib　**Arusha** アルーシャ（現在のタンザニアの都市。キリマンジャロから近い）　**refuel** 燃料を補給する　9 **get going** 出発する
11 **care about** ほしい
12 **had picked up the cot and carried it around the green tents...** 簡易ベッドを持って、緑のテントをまわって……
15 **consumed** 燃えてしまった　17 **once in** 一度中に入ると
18 **stuck...out** 突き出ていた　20 **clatter** プロペラの回り始めのときの音　21 **old** いつもの　**they** 飛行機に乗っているComptonと主人公。この場合、飛行機と考えていい　**swung around** むきを変えた　22 **Compie** Compton の愛称　**wart-hog** イボイノシシ（アフリカの野性のイノシシ）　23 **bumping** 揺れながら走っていく　**stretch** 直線コース　24 **the last bump rose** 最後のバウンドがあった　25 **flattening** 平たくなっていく。立体感をなくしていく　26 **clumps** 茂み　27 **game trails** 獣道　28 **waterholes** 水たまり、小さい池　**new water** 新しい水たまり

and the wildebeeste, big-headed dots seeming to climb as they moved in long fingers across the plain, now scattering as the shadow came toward them, they were tiny now, and the movement had no gallop, and the plain as far as you could see, gray-yellow now and ahead old Compie's tweed back and the brown felt hat. Then they were over the first hills and the wildebeeste were trailing up them, and then they were over mountains with sudden depths of green-rising forest and the solid bamboo slopes, and then the heavy forest again, sculptured into peaks and hollows until they crossed, and hills sloped down and then another plain, hot now, and purple brown, bumpy with heat and Compie looking back to see how he was riding. Then there were other mountains dark ahead.

And then instead of going on to Arusha they turned left, he evidently figured that they had the gas, and looking down he saw a pink sifting cloud, moving over the ground, and in the air, like the first snow in a blizzard, that comes from nowhere, and he knew the locusts were coming up from the South. Then they began to climb and they were going to the East it seemed, and then it darkened and they were in a storm, the rain so thick it seemed like flying through a waterfall, and then they were out and Compie turned his head and grinned and pointed and there, ahead, all he could see, as wide as all the world, great, high, and unbelievably white in the sun, was the square top of Kilimanjaro. And then he knew that there was where he was going.

The Snows of Kilimanjaro

1 **wildebeest** ヌー（アフリカに住む野牛） **big-headed dots** 大きな頭の点（頭の大きいヌーが点のように見える） **climb** 這う 2 **in long fingers** 細長い指のような列になって **scattering**（飛行機に驚いて）散っていく 3 **the shadow** 飛行機の影 4 **gallop** 全速力 8 **trailing up** のんびり登っていく 9 **green-rising forest** 大きく盛り上がった緑の森 10 **sculptured into** 地形が変わって〜になっていった 11 **hollows** 窪地、小渓谷 **until they crossed** やがてそのあたりを過ぎると 13 **bumpy with heat** 暑さのために揺れている（ように見える） 14 **how he was riding** ハリーがどんなふうか
17 **figured** 考えた 18 **sifting** ふるいを通して落ちてくるような 19 **blizzard** 吹雪 20 **locusts** バッタ 22 **it darkened** あたりが暗くなった 25 **grinned** ほほえんだ 28 **square** 四角い **he** 主人公

Just then the hyena stopped whimpering in the night and started to make a strange, human, almost crying sound. The woman heard it and stirred uneasily. She did not wake. In her dream she was at the house on Long Island and it was the night before her daughter's début. Somehow her father was there and he had been very rude. Then the noise the hyena made was so loud she woke and for a moment she did not know where she was and she was very afraid. Then she took the flashlight and shone it on the other cot that they had carried in after Harry had gone to sleep. She could see his bulk under the mosquito bar but somehow he had gotten his leg out and it hung down alongside the cot. The dressings had all come down and she could not look at it.

"Molo," she called, "Molo! Molo!"

Then she said, "Harry, Harry!" Then her voice rising, "Harry! Please. Oh Harry!"

There was no answer and she could not hear him breathing.

Outside the tent the hyena made the same strange noise that had awakened her. But she did not hear him for the beating of her heart.

2 **whimpering** 悲しげな鳴き声をあげる 4 **stirred uneasily** 胸騒ぎがした 5 **Long Island** ロングアイランド（ニューヨーク南東部の島） 6 **début** 社交界にデビューする 7 **Somehow** なぜか 8 **rude** 不作法な、無礼な 10 **flashlight** 懐中電灯 12 **bulk** 体 13 **mosquito bar** 蚊帳 **gotten his leg out** 脚を突きだしていた 14 **dressings** 包帯

The Short Happy Life of Francis Mocomber

It was now lunch time and they were all sitting under the double green fly of the dining tent pretending that nothing had happened.

"Will you have lime juice or lemon squash?" Macomber asked.

"I'll have a gimlet," Robert Wilson told him.

"I'll have a gimlet too. I need something," Macomber's wife said.

"I suppose it's the thing to do," Macomber agreed. "Tell him to make three gimlets."

The mess boy had started them already, lifting the bottles out of the canvas cooling bags that sweated wet in the wind that blew through the trees that shaded the tents.

"What had I ought to give them?" Macomber asked.

"A quid would be plenty," Wilson told him. "You don't want to spoil them."

"Will the headman distribute it?"

"Absolutely."

Francis Macomber had, half an hour before, been carried to his tent from the edge of the camp in triumph on the arms and shoulders of the cook, the personal boys, the skinner and the porters. The gun-bearers had taken no part in the demonstration. When the native boys put him down at the door of his tent, he had shaken all their hands, received their congratulations, and then gone into the tent and sat on the bed until his wife came in. She did not speak to him when she came in and he left the tent at once to wash his face and hands in the por-

2 **double green fly of the dining tent** 食事用テントの二重になっている緑色のフライ（フライシートのことで、テントの雨よけ・日よけ）

6 **gimlet** ギムレット（ジンベースのカクテル）

9 **the thing to do** やるべきこと

11 **mess boy** 食事係の少年　**the bottles** ジンのボトル

12 **sweated wet** 水滴で濡れている　13 **the trees that shaded the tents** テントに日陰を作っている木々

15 **What had I ought to give them?** 雇った者たちにチップをいくら払うべきだったのだろう？

16 **quid** ポンド（英国の通貨）の俗称　**plenty** 十分　17 **spoil** 甘やかす

18 **headman** リーダー　**distribute** 仲間に分ける

19 **Absolutely** もちろん

20 **half an hour before** これより三十分前に　21 **in triumph** 意気揚々と　**on the arms and shoulders** 手に持ったり肩に担いだりして　22 **personal boys** 雑用係の少年たち　23 **skinner** 動物の皮をはぐ係　**gun-bearers** 銃を運ぶ係　**had taken no part in the demonstration** その連中には加わらなかった　24 **native** 現地人の　25 **he had shaken all their hands** 全員と握手した

table wash basin outside and go over to the dining tent to sit in a comfortable canvas chair in the breeze and the shade.

"You've got your lion," Robert Wilson said to him, "and a damned fine one too."

Mrs. Macomber looked at Wilson quickly. She was an extremely handsome and well-kept woman of the beauty and social position which had, five years before, commanded five thousand dollars as the price of endorsing, with photographs, a beauty product which she had never used. She had been married to Francis Macomber for eleven years.

"He is a good lion, isn't he?" Macomber said. His wife looked at him now. She looked at both these men as though she had never seen them before.

One, Wilson, the white hunter, she knew she had never truly seen before. He was about middle height with sandy hair, a stubby mustache, a very red face and extremely cold blue eyes with faint white wrinkles at the corners that grooved merrily when he smiled. He smiled at her now and she looked away from his face at the way his shoulders sloped in the loose tunic he wore with the four big cartridges held in loops where the left breast pocket should have been, at his big brown hands, his old slacks, his very dirty boots and back to his red face again. She noticed where the baked red of his face stopped in a white line that marked the circle left by his Stetson hat that hung now from one of the pegs of the tent pole.

1 **wash basin** 洗面器
4 **You've got your lion** あなたはライオンを手に入れた　5 **a damned fine one** とても立派なライオン
7 **well-kept** スタイルのいい　**of the beauty and social position** 美しく社会的地位を持っている　9 **commanded as the price of endorsing** 広告料　10 **with photographs** 広告写真の　**a beauty product** 美容製品
15 **as though she had never seen them before** 初めて会ったかのように
16 **had never truly seen before** （じつは）今までじっくり見たことがなかった　18 **sandy** 薄茶色の　**stubby** 短く太い　**mustache** 口ひげ　20 **grooved** 深くなる　21 **looked away from his face at the way his shoulders sloped** 彼の顔から、なだらかな肩に視線を移した　23 **cartridges** カートリッジ、弾薬　**held in loops** 輪飾りにさしてある　**where the left breast pocket should have been** 左の胸ポケットがあるはずのところに　25 **slacks** ズボン　26 **baked red** 日焼けした赤い色　27 **the circle left by** 帽子の陰になって日焼けしていない輪の部分　28 **Stetson hat** ステットソン帽（カウボーイハット）

"Well, here's to the lion," Robert Wilson said. He smiled at her again and, not smiling, she looked curiously at her husband.

Francis Macomber was very tall, very well built if you did not mind that length of bone, dark, his hair cropped like an oarsman, rather thin-lipped, and was considered handsome. He was dressed in the same sort of safari clothes that Wilson wore except that his were new, he was thirty-five years old, kept himself very fit, was good at court games, had a number of biggame fishing records, and had just shown himself, very publicly, to be a coward.

"Here's to the lion," he said. "I can't ever thank you for what you did."

Margaret, his wife, looked away from him and back to Wilson.

"Let's not talk about the lion," she said.

Wilson looked over at her without smiling and now she smiled at him.

"It's been a very strange day," she said. "Hadn't you ought to put your hat on even under the canvas at noon? You told me that, you know."

"Might put it on," said Wilson.

"You know you have a very red face, Mr. Wilson," she told him and smiled again.

"Drink," said Wilson.

"I don't think so," she said. "Francis drinks a great deal, but his face is never red."

"It's red today," Macomber tried a joke.

1 **here's to the lion** ライオンに乾杯　2 **not smiling** 主語は彼女　**curiously** ものめずらしそうに

4 **well built** がっしりした体格　**if you did not mind that length of bone** 背が高すぎるのを気にしなければ　5 **dark** 肌が浅黒い

6 **cropped** 短く刈った　**oarsman** ボート選手　9 **kept himself very fit** 体調を最上の状態に保つ　10 **court games** コートを使う球技　**biggame** 大きな獲物　11 **had just shown himself, very publicly** 人前で派手にさらしてしまった（この場面以前のできごとに関してのことで、このあと、内容が明らかになっていく）　12 **coward** 臆病者

13 **I can't ever thank you** いくら感謝しても足りない

21 **canvas** キャンバス地のテント

23 **Might put it on** 帽子をかぶったほうがいい

26 **Drink** 酒のせい

29 **It's red today** 臆病ぶりをさらして恥をかいたために赤面しているという意味　**tried a joke** 冗談っぽくいってみた

"No," said Margaret. "It's mine that's red today. But Mr. Wilson's is always red."

"Must be racial" said Wilson. "I say, you wouldn't like to drop my beauty as a topic, would you?"

"I've just started on it."

"Let's chuck it," said Wilson.

"Conversation is going to be so difficult," Margaret said.

"Don't be silly, Margot," her husband said.

"No difficulty," Wilson said. "Got a damn fine lion."

Margot looked at them both and they both saw that she was going to cry. Wilson had seen it coming for a long time and he dreaded it. Macomber was past dreading it.

"I wish it hadn't happened. Oh, I wish it hadn't happened," she said and started for her tent. She made no noise of crying but they could see that her shoulders were shaking under the rose-colored, sun-proofed shirt she wore.

"Women upset," said Wilson to the tall man. "Amounts to nothing. Strain on the nerves and one thing'n another."

"No," said Macomber. "I suppose that I rate that for the rest of my life now."

"Nonsense. Let's have a spot of the giant killer," said Wilson. "Forget the whole thing. Nothing to it anyway."

"We might try," said Macomber. "I won't forget what you did for me though."

"Nothing," said Wilson. "All nonsense."

3 **racial** 人種的なもの **I say** あのね（相手の注意を喚起する表現） 4 **drop my beauty as a topic** わたしの美貌を話の種からはずす

5 **I've just started on it** 今その話を始めたばかりよ

6 **chuck** やめる

9 **Margot** マーゴ（マーガレットの別称）

10 **Got a damn fine lion** すばらしいライオンを手に入れたんだから

12 **had seen it coming** マーガレットが泣きだすことはわかっていた 13 **dread** 恐れていた **past dreading it** 恐れている以上だった

15 **I wish it hadon't happened** あんなことが起こらなければよかったのに（具体的な内容はそのうち明らかになる） 16 **started for her tent** 自分のテントに向かった 18 **sun-proofed** 日差しを通さない厚手の

20 **Women upset** 女はすぐに感情的になる **the tall man** 背の高い男（マカンバーのこと） 21 **Amounts to nothing** たいしたことではない **Strains on the nerves** 精神的なストレス **and one thing'n another** その他、いろいろ（'n は and の省略形）

23 **rate that** 妻にああいう態度をとられつづける（rate ＝〜するに値する）

25 **have a spot** 一杯飲む **giant killer** 強い酒 26 **Nothing to it** なんてことはない

So they sat there in the shade where the camp was pitched under some wide-topped acacia trees with a boulder-strewn cliff behind them, and a stretch of grass that ran to the bank of a boulder-filled stream in front with forest beyond it, and drank their just-cool lime drinks and avoided one another's eyes while the boys set the table for lunch. Wilson could tell that the boys all knew about it now and when he saw Macomber's personal boy looking curiously at his master while he was putting dishes on the table he snapped at him in Swahili. The boy turned away with his face blank.

"What were you telling him?" Macomber asked.

"Nothing. Told him to look alive or I'd see he got about fifteen of the best."

"What's that? Lashes?"

"It's quite illegal," Wilson said. "You're supposed to fine them."

"Do you still have them whipped?"

"Oh, yes. They could raise a row if they chose to complain. But they don't. They prefer it to the fines."

"How strange!" said Macomber.

"Not strange, really," Wilson said. "Which would you rather do? Take a good birching or lose your pay?"

Then he felt embarrassed at asking it and before Macomber could answer he went on, "We all take a beating every day, you know, one way or another."

This was no better. "Good God," he thought. "I am a diplomat, aren't I?"

"Yes, we take a beating," said Macomber, still not

2 **pitched** 設営されている　**wide-topped** 上が広がっている **acacia trees** アカシアの木々　3 **boulder-strewn cliff** あちこちに大きな岩の突き出た崖　4 **boulder-filled stream** 岩のごろごろした川　5 **just-cool** ちょうどよく冷えた　7 **tell** 気づく　8 **it** マカンバーが臆病ぶりをさらしたできごと　10 **snapped** 怒鳴る　**Swahili** スワヒリ語　11 **with his face blank** 無表情な顔で　13 **look alive** てきぱきする　14 **the best** =the best of whipping（強烈な鞭打ち）

15 **Lashes** 鞭

16 **You're supposed to fine** 本来なら罰金を科すことになっている（you は一般人称）

18 **have them whipped** 鞭で打たせる

19 **raise a row** 騒ぎを起こす　**chose to complain** 不満を表に出す気なら　20 **it** 鞭打ち

23 **birching** 鞭打ち

24 **felt embarrassed** 気まずくなった　25 **take a beating** 鞭打ちを受ける　26 **one way or another** なんらかの形で

27 **Good God** おいおい　**he thought** この部分はウィルスンの考えていること　28 **diplomat**（外交官から転じて）口がうまい人

looking at him. "I'm awfully sorry about that lion business. It doesn't have to go any further, does it? I mean no one will hear about it, will they?"

"You mean will I tell it at the Mathaiga Club?" Wilson looked at him now coldly. He had not expected this. So he's a bloody four-letter man as well as a bloody coward, he thought. I rather liked him too until today. But how is one to know about an American?

"No," said Wilson. "I'm a professional hunter. We never talk about our clients. You can be quite easy on that. It's supposed to be bad form to ask us not to talk though."

He had decided now that to break would be much easier. He would eat, then, by himself and could read a book with his meals. They would eat by themselves. He would see them through the safari on a very formal basis——what was it the French called it? Distinguished consideration——and it would be a damn sight easier than having to go through this emotional trash. He'd insult him and make a good clean break. Then he could read a book with his meals and he'd still be drinking their whisky. That was the phrase for it when a safari went bad. You ran into another white hunter and you asked, "How is everything going?" and he answered, "Oh, I'm still drinking their whisky," and you knew everything had gone to pot.

"I'm sorry," Macomber said and looked at him with his American face that would stay adolescent until it became middle-aged, and Wilson noted his crew-cropped

1 **awfully** とても　**that lion business** あのライオンの件　2 **It doesn't have to go any further** これ以上話が広まるはずがない　3 **no one will hear about it** だれもこの話を耳にすることはない　4 **the Mathaiga Club** マサイガ・クラブ（社交クラブの名）　6 **bloody** ひどく　**four-letter** どうしようもない（damn、fuck、shitなど、英単語に四文字の汚い言葉が多いことから）　8 **how is one to know about an American?** アメリカ人なんてわからない（oneは一般人称）

9 **professional hunter** ハンティングのガイド　10 **quite easy** まったく心配いらない　11 **bad form** 無作法　13 **break** つきあいをやめる　14 **then** つきあいをやめれば　15 **They** マカンバー夫妻　16 **safari** サファリ旅行　**formal basis** うわべだけの形式的な態度で　17 **what was it the French called it?** あるフランス人が言った表現を思い出そうとしている　**Distinguished consideration** 品位ある配慮　18 **a damn sight** はるかに（easierを強調している）　19 **emotional trash** 感情的なごたごた　20 **make a good clean break** さっぱり別れる　22 **the phrase for it** ハンティングのガイドの間でサファリ客とうまくいっていないときに使われる表現　23 **ran into** ばったり出会う　26 **had gone to pot** まずい状態になっている　28 **adolescent** 十代のように青臭い　29 **noted** しげしげと見た　**crew-cropped** 短く刈った

hair, fine eyes only faintly shifty, good nose, thin lips and handsome jaw. "I'm sorry I didn't realize that. There are lots of things I don't know."

So what could he do, Wilson thought. He was all ready to break it off quickly and neatly and here the beggar was apologizing after he had just insulted him. He made one more attempt. "Don't worry about me talking," he said. "I have a living to make. You know in Africa no woman ever misses her lion and no white man ever bolts."

"I bolted like a rabbit," Macomber said.

Now what in hell were you going to do about a man who talked like that, Wilson wondered.

Wilson looked at Macomber with his flat, blue, machine-gunner's eyes and the other smiled back at him. He had a pleasant smile if you did not notice how his eyes showed when he was hurt.

"Maybe I can fix it up on buffalo," he said. "We're after them next, aren't we?"

"In the morning if you like," Wilson told him. Perhaps he had been wrong. This was certainly the way to take it. You most certainly could not tell a damned thing about an American. He was all for Macomber again. If you could forget the morning. But, of course, you couldn't. The morning had been about as bad as they come.

"Here comes the Memsahib," he said. She was walking over from her tent looking refreshed and cheerful and quite lovely. She had a very perfect oval face,

1 **only faintly shifty** どことなくずるそうな
5 **break it off** つきあいを絶つ　6 **beggar** 哀れなやつ　7 **about me talking** わたしが口外するなんていうことは　8 **I have a living to make** 食っていかなくてはならない　9 **misses her lion** 狙ったライオンを打ち損ねる　10 **bolts** 逃げだす
12 **in hell** いったい（強調）
14 **flat** きっぱりとした　**machine-gunner's eyes** 機関銃を撃つ男のような目　15 **the other** マカンバー　16 **if you did not notice** 気がつかなければ　**how his eyes showed when he was hurt** 傷ついているときの彼の目の表情
18 **fix it up** 挽回する　**We're after them** バッファローを狩りに行く
20 **In the morning** 明日の朝　21 **the way to take it** 取るべき態度　22 **could not tell a damned thing about an American** アメリカ人というやつはわけがわからない　23 **was all for** 〜に好意的になった　24 **the morning** その日の朝のできごと　25 **as bad as they come** 実際、本当にひどいことが起きた
27 **Memsahib** スワヒリ語で女性に対する敬称。英語の lady にあたる　29 **oval** 卵形の

so perfect that you expected her to be stupid. But she wasn't stupid, Wilson thought, no, not stupid.

"How is the beautiful red-faced Mr. Wilson? Are you feeling better, Francis, my pearl?"

"Oh, much," said Macomber.

"I've dropped the whole thing," she said, sitting down at the table.

"What importance is there to whether Francis is any good at killing lions? That's not his trade. That's Mr. Wilson's trade. Mr. Wilson is really very impressive killing anything. You do kill anything, don't you?"

"Oh, anything," said Wilson. "Simply anything." They are, he thought, the hardest in the world; the hardest, the cruelest, the most predatory and the most attractive and their men have softened or gone to pieces nervously as they have hardened. Or is it that they pick men they can handle? They can't know that much at the age they marry, he thought. He was grateful that he had gone through his education on American women before now because this was a very attractive one.

"We're going after buff in the morning," he told her.

"I'm coming," she said.

"No, you're not."

"Oh, yes, I am. Mayn't I, Francis?"

"Why not stay in camp?"

"Not for anything," she said. "I wouldn't miss something like today for anything."

When she left, Wilson was thinking, when she went off to cry, she seemed a hell of a fine woman. She

4 **my pearl** わたしの大切な人
5 **much** とても（気分がよくなった）
6 **I've dropped the whole thing** 水に流すことにした
9 **trade** 職業　10 **impressive** すばらしい　11 **You do kill anything, don't you?** あなたはどんなものでも殺すんでしょう？
13 **They** こういう女たち　**the hardest** 最高に手ごわい
14 **predatory** 貪欲な　15 **their men** 夫たち　**softened** 軟弱になる　**gone to pieces nervously** 神経がぼろぼろになる
16 **hardened** 厳しくなる　**Or is it that** あるいは、～ということなのか　**pick** 選ぶ　17 **can't know that much** そこまでわかっているはずがない　18 **had gone through his education on American women** アメリカ女を経験して学んでいる　19 **before now** すでに　20 **attractive one** 魅力的な女
21 **buff** バッファロー
23 **No, you're not** ウィルスンがマーガレットの同行に反対している
24 **Mayn't I** いいでしょう？
26 **Not for anything** ぜったいにいや　**I wouldn't miss something like today for anything** 今日みたいなできごとを見逃すのは、ぜったいにいや
29 **a hell of** ものすごく

seemed to understand, to realize, to be hurt for him and for herself and to know how things really stood. She is away for twenty minutes and now she is back, simply enamelled in that American female cruelty. They are the damnedest women. Really the damnedest.

"We'll put on another show for you tomorrow," Francis Macomber said.

"You're not coming," Wilson said.

"You're very mistaken," she told him. "And I want so to see you perform again. You were lovely this morning. That is if blowing things' heads off is lovely."

"Here's the lunch," said Wilson. "You're very merry, aren't you?"

"Why not? I didn't come out here to be dull."

"Well, it hasn't been dull," Wilson said. He could see the boulders in the river and the high bank beyond with the trees and he remembered the morning.

"Oh, no," she said. "It's been charming. And tomorrow. You don't know how I look forward to tomorrow."

"That's eland he's offering you," Wilson said.

"They're the big cowy things that jump like hares, aren't they?"

"I suppose that describes them," Wilson said.

"It's very good meat," Macomber said.

"Did you shoot it, Francis?" she asked.

"Yes."

"They're not dangerous, are they?"

"Only if they fall on you," Wilson told her.

"I'm so glad."

1 **to be hurt for him and for herself** 彼と同じように自分も傷ついている 2 **know how things really stood** 状況を理解している (things は「状況」) 4 **enamelled** 塗り固められている
5 **damnedest** とてもひどい
6 **put on another show** またおもしろいものを見せてやる
10 **perform** いいところを見せる、活躍する 11 **That is if blowing things' heads off is lovely** 動物の頭を吹き飛ばすのが素晴らしいとしたら
14 **dull** 退屈
16 **boulders** 岩
19 **look forward to** 〜を楽しみにしている
20 **That** 皿にのっている料理　**eland** エランド、イランド (アフリカに生息するレイヨウ)
21 **cowy things** ウシのような動物　**hares** 野ウサギ
23 **that describes them** そんな感じですかね
28 **they fall on you** 動物が襲いかかってくる (you は一般人称)

"Why not let up on the bitchery just a little, Margot," Macomber said, cutting the eland steak and putting some mashed potato, gravy and carrot on the down-turned fork that tined through the piece of meat.

"I suppose I could," she said, "since you put it so prettily."

"Tonight we'll have champagne for the lion," Wilson said. "It's a bit too hot at noon."

"Oh, the lion," Margot said. "I'd forgotten the lion!"

So, Robert Wilson thought to himself, she *is* giving him a ride, isn't she? Or do you suppose that's her idea of putting up a good show? How should a woman act when she discovers her husband is a bloody coward? She's damn cruel but they're all cruel. They govern, of course, and to govern one has to be cruel sometimes. Still, I've seen enough of their damn terrorism.

"Have some more eland," he said to her politely.

That afternoon, late, Wilson and Macomber went out in the motor car with the native driver and the two gun-bearers. Mrs. Macomber stayed in the camp. It was too hot to go out, she said, and she was going with them in the early morning. As they drove off Wilson saw her standing under the big tree, looking pretty rather than beautiful in her faintly rosy khaki, her dark hair drawn back off her forehead and gathered in a knot low on her neck, her face as fresh, he thought, as though she were in England. She waved to them as the car went off through the swale of high grass and curved around through the trees into the small hills of orchard bush.

1 **Why not let up on the bitchery** 嫌味を言うのはやめてくれ
3 **down-turned fork** 下向きになったフォーク   4 **tined through** 突き刺した
5 **I could** あとに let up on the bichery が省略されている   **since you put it so prettily** あなたがとても感じのいい頼み方をしてくれたから（これ自体が嫌味になっている）
10 **thought to himself** 胸の内で思った   **giving him a ride** 夫を侮辱する   12 **putting up good show** おもしろいものを演じる   14 **they're all** 女というものはみんな   **govern** （男を）支配する   16 **I've seen enough of their damn terrorism** 女たちの暴虐なふるまいをさんざん見てきた
19 **motor car** 自動車   22 **the early morning** 翌日の早朝   23 **pretty rather than beautiful** 美しいというよりかわいらしい   24 **in her faintly rosy khaki** バラ色を帯びたカーキ色の服を着て   **drawn back off her forehead** 髪を後ろになでつけて額を出している   25 **knot** 髪を束ねた部分   28 **swale of high grass** 高い草のはえた湿地   29 **orchard bush** 広大なサバンナ

In the orchard bush they found a herd of impala, and leaving the car they stalked one old ram with long, wide-spread horns and Macomber killed it with a very creditable shot that knocked the buck down at a good two hundred yards and sent the herd off bounding wildly and leaping over one another's backs in long, leg-drawn-up leaps as unbelievable and as floating as those one makes sometimes in dreams.

"That was a good shot," Wilson said. "They're a small target."

"Is it a worth-while head?" Macomber asked.

"It's excellent," Wilson told him. "You shoot like that and you'll have no trouble."

"Do you think we'll find buffalo tomorrow?"

"There's a good chance of it. They feed out early in the morning and with luck we may catch them in the open."

"I'd like to clear away that lion business," Macomber said. "It's not very pleasant to have your wife see you do something like that."

I should think it would be even more unpleasant to do it, Wilson thought, wife or no wife, or to talk about it having done it. But he said, "I wouldn't think about that any more. Anyone could be upset by his first lion. That's all over."

But that night after dinner and a whisky and soda by the fire before going to bed, as Francis Macomber lay on his cot with the mosquito bar over him and listened to the night noises it was not all over. It was neither all

1 **a herd** 群れ　**impala** インパラ　2 **stalked** 追った　**ram** インパラのこと　4 **creditable** 危なげのない　**buck** インパラのこと　**at a good two hundred yards** たっぷり200ヤード（1ヤードは0.9メートル）離れた地点から　5 **bounding** 跳びはねる　6 **over one another's backs** たがいの背を飛びこえて　**leg-drawn-up leaps** 脚を深く曲げる跳び方　7 **floating** 宙に浮く　**those** =leaps　8 **one makes sometimes in dreams** 夢に出てくるインパラがときおり見せるような

9 **That** インパラをしとめた一発を指す

11 **a worth-while head** 価値のある頭部（獲物の頭部をハンティングの記念品にする）

12 **You shoot like that and you'll have no trouble** あんなふうに撃てば、失敗することはない

15 **There's a good chance** 可能性は十分ある　**feed out** 草を食む　17 **open** まわりに障害物がなくて、見通しの利くところ

18 **clear away** 払拭する

21 **I should think** 自分なら〜と思う　**to do it** そんなことをすること（人に話すこと）　22 **wife or no wife** 妻がいようがいまいが　**talk about it having done it** 自分の失敗を人に話すこと

24 **That's all over** もうすべて終わったことだ

26 **a whisky and soda** ウィスキーのソーダ割り　28 **cot** 簡易ベッド　**mosquito bar** 蚊帳　29 **it was not all over** 終わっていなかった

over nor was it beginning. It was there exactly as it happened with some parts of it indelibly emphasized and he was miserably ashamed at it. But more than shame he felt cold, hollow fear in him. The fear was still there like a cold slimy hollow in all the emptiness where once his confidence had been and it made him feel sick. It was still there with him now.

It had started the night before when he had wakened and heard the lion roaring somewhere up along the river. It was a deep sound and at the end there were sort of coughing grunts that made him seem just outside the tent, and when Francis Macomber woke in the night to hear it he was afraid. He could hear his wife breathing quietly, asleep. There was no one to tell he was afraid, nor to be afraid with him, and, lying alone, he did not know the Somali proverb that says a brave man is always frightened three times by a lion; when he first sees his track, when he first hears him roar and when he first confronts him. Then while they were eating breakfast by lantern light out in the dining tent, before the sun was up, the lion roared again and Francis thought he was just at the edge of camp.

"Sounds like an old-timer," Robert Wilson said, looking up from his kippers and coffee. "Listen to him cough."

"Is he very close?"

"A mile or so up the stream."

"Will we see him?"

"We'll have a look."

1 **It was there exactly as it happened** 起きたときのまま記憶に残っている 2 **with some parts of it indelibly emphasized** 一部は消しようがないほど強調されて 4 **hollow** 空虚な 5 **slimy** ぬるぬるした **all the emptiness where once his confidence had been** かつて自信が存在していた（自信を失ってできてしまった）空洞 6 **feel sick** 吐き気がする

8 **the night before** 前の晩（恥をかいたできごとの前夜） 11 **grunts** うなり声 **made him seem just outside the tent** ライオンがテントのすぐ外にいるように感じさせた 15 **nor to be afraid with him** 恐怖を分かちあう相手もいなかった 16 **Somali** ソマリ族（アフリカ東部に住む部族）の **proverb that says** 〜ということわざ 17 **he first sees his track** 勇者が初めてライオンの足跡を見るとき（heは勇者で、hisはライオン） 19 **confronts** 向かいあう 20 **lantern** ランタン 21 **he was just at the edge of camp** ライオンがキャンプの端まで来ていた 23 **old-timer** 年寄り（のライオン） 24 **kippers** 燻製の魚 29 **We'll have a look** 探しにいこう

"Does his roaring carry that far? It sounds as though he were right in camp."

"Carries a hell of a long way," said Robert Wilson. "It's strange the way it carries. Hope he's a shootable cat. The boys said there was a very big one about here."

"If I get a shot, where should I hit him," Macomber asked, "to stop him?"

"In the shoulders," Wilson said. "In the neck if you can make it. Shoot for bone. Break him down."

"I hope I can place it properly," Macomber said.

"You shoot very well," Wilson told him. "Take your time. Make sure of him. The first one in is the one that counts."

"What range will it be?"

"Can't tell. Lion has something to say about that. Don't shoot unless it's close enough so you can make sure."

"At under a hundred yards?" Macomber asked.

Wilson looked at him quickly.

"Hundred's about right. Might have to take him a bit under. Shouldn't chance a shot at much over that. A hundred's a decent range. You can hit him wherever you want at that. Here comes the Memsahib."

"Good morning," she said. "Are we going after that lion?"

"As soon as you deal with your breakfast," Wilson said. "How are you feeling?"

"Marvellous," she said. "I'm very excited."

"I'll just go and see that everything is ready." Wilson

1 **carry that far** これほど遠くまで届く
3 **a hell of** ものすごく　4 **the way it carries** 声の伝わり方　**shootable** 撃つことのできる（妊娠している雌ライオンなどは撃つことを禁止されている）
6 **get a shot** 獲物が射程距離に入ったら
9 **shoot for bone** 骨を狙って撃つ　**Break him down** ライオンを仕留める
10 **place** ねらったところに撃ちこむ
11 **Take your time** 焦らずにやる　12 **Make sure of him** 確実に命中させる　**The first one in** 最初に命中する弾丸　13 **counts** 重要だ
14 **What range will it be** 距離はどのくらいだろう
15 **Can't tell** はっきりとはわからない　**Lion has something to say about that** それについてはライオンにも言い分がある（ライオンによりけり）
20 **Hundred's** Hundred は 100 ヤード　**about right** ほぼ適切だ　**take him a bit under** もう少し近くに引きよせてから撃つ
21 **Shouldn't chance a shot** 運まかせに撃ってはいけない　**at much over that** それよりはるかに遠いところで　22 **decent** 適正な　23 **at that** その距離なら
26 **deal with** すませる

went off. As he left the lion roared again.

"Noisy beggar," Wilson said. "We'll put a stop to that."

"What's the matter, Francis?" his wife asked him.

"Nothing," Macomber said.

"Yes, there is," she said. "What are you upset about?"

"Nothing," he said.

"Tell me," she looked at him. "Don't you feel well?"

"It's that damned roaring," he said. "It's been going on all night, you know."

"Why didn't you wake me," she said. "I'd love to have heard it."

"I've got to kill the damned thing," Macomber said, miserably.

"Well, that's what you're out here for, isn't it?"

"Yes. But I'm nervous. Hearing the thing roar gets on my nerves."

"Well then, as Wilson said, kill him and stop his roaring."

"Yes, darling," said Francis Macomber. "It sounds easy, doesn't it?"

"You're not afraid, are you?"

"Of course not. But I'm nervous from hearing him roar all night."

"You'll kill him marvellously," she said. "I know you will. I'm awfully anxious to see it."

"Finish your breakfast and we'll be starting."

"It's not light yet," she said. "This is a ridiculous hour."

2 **Noisy beggar** うるさいやつ（ライオンを指す）　**put a stop to that** 吠えるのをやめさせる
6 **Yes, there is** そんなわけないわ（夫が Nothing と言ったのに対して）
9 **damned** いまいましい
13 **got to kill** 殺さなければならない　14 **miserably** みじめっぽく
15 **that's what you're out here for** そのためにここにいる
16 **the thing** あのライオン　**gets on my nerve** 神経にさわる
20 **It sounds easy** 簡単なように聞こえる
26 **awfully anxious** したくてたまらない
28 **light**（日が昇って）明るくなっている　**ridiculous hour** 出かけるには変な時間

Just then the lion roared in a deep-chested moaning, suddenly guttural, ascending vibration that seemed to shake the air and ended in a sigh and a heavy, deep-chested grunt.

"He sounds almost here," Macomber's wife said.

"My God," said Macomber. "I hate that damned noise."

"It's very impressive."

"Impressive. It's frightful."

Robert Wilson came up then carrying his short, ugly, shockingly bigbored .505 Gibbs and grinning.

"Come on," he said. "Your gun-bearer has your Springfield and the big gun. Everything's in the car. Have you solids?"

"Yes."

"I'm ready," Mrs. Macomber said.

"Must make him stop that racket," Wilson said. "You get in front. The Memsahib can sit back here with me."

They climbed into the motor car and, in the gray first daylight, moved off up the river through the trees. Macomber opened the breech of his rifle and saw he had metal-cased bullets, shut the bolt and put the rifle on safety. He saw his hand was trembling. He felt in his pocket for more cartridges and moved his fingers over the cartridges in the loops of his tunic front. He turned back to where Wilson sat in the rear seat of the doorless, box-bodied motor car beside his wife, them both grinning with excitement, and Wilson leaned forward and whispered,

1 **deep-chested moaning** 胸の奥底から出るようなうめき声 2 **guttural** しわがれた声 **ascending vibration** 高まる振動 3 **sigh** 吐息 4 **grunt** うなり声
8 **impressive** 立派な、印象的な
11 **bigbored .505 Gibbs** 大口径の.505 ギブズ銃 **grinning** にやにやしながら
13 **Springfield** スプリングフィールド銃 14 **solids** 弾丸
17 **racket** 騒ぎ（ライオンの声） 18 **get in front** 前の席に乗る
21 **breech** 銃身後尾 22 **metal-cased bullets** 被甲弾（真鍮などの金属で覆われた弾丸） **bolt** 遊底（薬室の後ろをブロックする部品。ボルトハンドルで操作する） **put the rifle on safety** ライフルの安全装置をかける 23 **felt in his pocket for more cartridges** ポケットをさわってそこにも弾薬があるのを確かめる 25 **the loops of his tunic front** 上着の前につけた輪飾り
26 **rear seat** 後部座席 27 **box-bodied** 箱形の

"See the birds dropping. Means the old boy has left his kill."

On the far bank of the stream Macomber could see, above the trees, vultures circling and plummeting down.

"Chances are he'll come to drink along here," Wilson whispered. "Before he goes to lay up. Keep an eye out."

They were driving slowly along the high bank of the stream which here cut deeply to its boulder-filled bed, and they wound in and out through big trees as they drove. Macomber was watching the opposite bank when he felt Wilson take hold of his arm. The car stopped.

"There he is," he heard the whisper. "Ahead and to the right. Get out and take him. He's a marvellous lion."

Macomber saw the lion now. He was standing almost broadside, his great head up and turned toward them. The early morning breeze that blew toward them was just stirring his dark mane, and the lion looked huge, silhouetted on the rise of bank in the gray morning light, his shoulders heavy, his barrel of a body bulking smoothly.

"How far is he?" asked Macomber, raising his rifle.

"About seventy-five. Get out and take him."

"Why not shoot from where I am?"

"You don't shoot them from cars," he heard Wilson saying in his ear. "Get out. He's not going to stay there all day."

Macomber stepped out of the curved opening at the side of the front seat, onto the step and down onto the ground. The lion still stood looking majestically and

1 **dropping** 空から舞い降りてきている　**Means** 前に That を補う。ということは〜を意味する　**old boy** 老いぼれ（ライオンのこと）　**left his kill** 獲物を食べ残していった
4 **vultures** ハゲワシ　**plummeting** 急降下してくる
5 **Chances are** 〜の可能性がある　6 **lay up** 寝る　**Keep an eye out** 見張っておくように
9 **wound in and out through** を縫うように進んだ
15 **broadside** 側面をこちらに向けて　17 **mane** たてがみ
18 **silhouetted** 輪郭が浮かびあがる　**rise of bank** 川岸の高くなった部分　19 **barrel** 胴体　**bulking smoothly** ゆるやかにふくらんでいる
27 **curved opening** 半円形の出入り口　29 **majestically** 堂々と

coolly toward this object that his eyes only showed in silhouette, bulking like some super-rhino. There was no man smell carried toward him and he watched the object, moving his great head a little from side to side. Then watching the object, not afraid, but hesitating before going down the bank to drink with such a thing opposite him, he saw a man figure detach itself from it and he turned his heavy head and swung away toward the cover of the trees as he heard a cracking crash and felt the slam of a .30-06 220-grain solid bullet that bit his flank and ripped in sudden hot scalding nausea through his stomach. He trotted, heavy, bigfooted, swinging wounded full-bellied, through the trees toward the tall grass and cover, and the crash came again to go past him ripping the air apart. Then it crashed again and he felt the blow as it hit his lower ribs and ripped on through, blood sudden hot and frothy in his mouth, and he galloped toward the high grass where he could crouch and not be seen and make them bring the crashing thing close enough so he could make a rush and get the man that held it.

Macomber had not thought how the lion felt as he got out of the car. He only knew his hands were shaking and as he walked away from the car it was almost impossible for him to make his legs move. They were stiff in the thighs, but he could feel the muscles fluttering. He raised the rifle, sighted on the junction of the lion's head and shoulders and pulled the trigger. Nothing happened though he pulled until he thought his finger

1 **coolly** 冷静に **this object** ライオンから見た車のこと **his eyes only showed in silhouette** ライオンの目には輪郭しか映っていない 2 **bulking** 大きい **super-rhino** 巨大なサイ 5 **hesitating before going down** おりていくのをためらって 7 **detach** 離れる **it** 車 8 **swung away** 体の向きを変えた 9 **cover of the trees** 隠れられるような木々 **cracking crash** 弾けるような音（銃声のこと） 10 **slam** 衝撃 **.30-06 220-grain** .30-06口径の銃が発した220グレイン（1グレインは0.0648グラム）の弾丸 **solid** 強力な **bit** めりこむ（biteの過去形） 11 **flank** 横腹 **ripped in** 引き裂いて〜した **scalding nausea** 焼けつくような吐き気 12 **trotted** 駆ける **bigfooted** 大きな足で 13 **wounded full-bellied** 大きな腹に傷を負って 14 **cover** 身を隠せるところ 15 **ripping the air apart** 空気を引き裂いて 16 **ribs** 肋骨 **ripped on** 引き裂いた 17 **frothy** 泡立つ 18 **crouch** 身を伏せる 19 **make them bring the crashing thing** やつらにあの轟音を発する物体を持ってこさせる 20 **make a rush** すばやく飛びかかる **get the man that held it** 銃を持っている男を仕留める

22 **had not thought** 考えてもいなかった 25 **stiff** こわばる 26 **thighs** 太もも **fluttering** ふるえている 27 **sighted** 狙いを定める **junction of the lion's head and shoulders** ライオンの頭と肩がつながっているところ 29 **until his finger would break** 指の骨が折れそうになるまで

would break. Then he knew he had the safety on and as he lowered the rifle to move the safety over he moved another frozen pace forward, and the lion seeing his silhouette flow clear of the silhouette of the car, turned and started off at a trot, and, as Macomber fired, he heard a whunk that meant that the bullet was home; but the lion kept on going. Macomber shot again and every one saw the bullet throw a spout of dirt beyond the trotting lion. He shot again, remembering to lower his aim, and they all heard the bullet hit, and the lion went into a gallop and was in the tall grass before he had the bolt pushed forward.

Macomber stood there feeling sick at his stomach, his hands that held the Springfield still cocked, shaking, and his wife and Robert Wilson were standing by him. Beside him too were the two gun-bearers chattering in Wakamba.

"I hit him," Macomber said. "I hit him twice."

"You gut-shot him and you hit him somewhere forward," Wilson said without enthusiasm. The gun-bearers looked very grave. They were silent now.

"You may have killed him," Wilson went on. "We'll have to wait a while before we go in to find out."

"What do you mean?"

"Let him get sick before we follow him up."

"Oh," said Macomber.

"He's a hell of a fine lion," Wilson said cheerfully. "He's gotten into a bad place though."

"Why is it bad?"

1 **safety on** 安全装置をかけてある　2 **move safety over** 安全装置をはずす　**moved another frozen pace** こわばった脚でもう一歩踏みだした　4 **flow clear of the silhouette of the car** 車の輪郭からマカンバーの影が流れるように離れる（ライオンの視点からの描写）　6 **whunk** 弾丸が当たった音　**home** 命中する　8 **throw a spout of dirt** 土をはねあげた　**beyond** ライオンのむこう　9 **lower his aim** 低目にねらいを定める　11 **before he had the bolt pushed forward** ボルトハンドルを（引いて）前に押しもどすまえに
14 **cocked** 撃鉄を起こした状態で（いつでも撃てる状態で）
17 **Wakamba** カンバ語（カンバ族はケニアに住む部族）
19 **gut-shot** 腹に命中させた　**somewhere forward** 体の前のあたり　21 **grave** 真剣な
25 **Let him get sick** ライオンを弱らせておく

"Can't see him until you're on him."

"Oh," said Macomber.

"Come on," said Wilson. "The Memsahib can stay here in the car. We'll go to have a look at the blood spoor."

"Stay here, Margot," Macomber said to his wife. His mouth was very dry and it was hard for him to talk.

"Why?" she asked.

"Wilson says to."

"We're going to have a look," Wilson said. "You stay here. You can see even better from here."

"All right."

Wilson spoke in Swahili to the driver. He nodded and said, "Yes, Bwana."

Then they went down the steep bank and across the stream, climbing over and around the boulders and up the other bank, pulling up by some projecting roots, and along it until they found where the lion had been trotting when Macomber first shot. There was dark blood on the short grass that the gun-bearers pointed out with grass stems, and that ran away behind the river bank trees.

"What do we do?" asked Macomber.

"Not much choice," said Wilson. "We can't bring the car over. Bank's too steep. We'll let him stiffen up a bit and then you and I'll go in and have a look for him."

"Can't we set the grass on fire?" Macomber asked.

"Too green."

"Can't we send beaters?"

Wilson looked at him appraisingly. "Of course we

1 **you're on him** 近くにいって向かい合う

5 **spoor** 跡

14 **Bwana** スワヒリ語で男性に対する敬称。英語の sir とか master にあたる

16 **climbing over and around the boulders** 岩を乗り越えたりまわりこんだりして   17 **pulling up by** 〜につかまって体を引きあげて   **projecting roots** 地上に突き出ている木の根   21 **ran away** (血の跡は) 〜に向かって続いていた

24 **stiffen up** 硬直する   25 **go in** (ライオンが隠れている草むらに) 入っていく

28 **beaters** 勢子 (草をたたいたり、音を立てたりして獲物を追いだす役の人)

29 **appraisingly** 値踏みするように

can," he said. "But it's just a touch murderous. You see, we know the lion's wounded. You can drive an unwounded lion——he'll move on ahead of a noise——but a wounded lion's going to charge. You can't see him until you're right on him. He'll make himself perfectly flat in cover you wouldn't think would hide a hare. You can't very well send boys in there to that sort of a show. Somebody bound to get mauled."

"What about the gun-bearers?"

"Oh, they'll go with us. It's their *shauri*. You see, they signed on for it. They don't look too happy though, do they?"

"I don't want to go in there," said Macomber. It was out before he knew he'd said it.

"Neither do I," said Wilson very cheerily. "Really no choice though." Then, as an afterthought, he glanced at Macomber and saw suddenly how he was trembling and the pitiful look on his face.

"You don't have to go in, of course," he said. "That's what I'm hired for, you know. That's why I'm so expensive."

"You mean you'd go in by yourself? Why not leave him there?"

Robert Wilson, whose entire occupation had been with the lion and the problem he presented, and who had not been thinking about Macomber except to note that he was rather windy, suddenly felt as though he had opened the wrong door in a hotel and seen something shameful.

1 **a touch murderous** ちょっとあぶない　2 **drive** 追い立てる　3 **ahead of a noise** 音と反対方向に　4 **charge** 飛びかかる
5 **right on him** すぐ近くに　**perfectly flat** ぴったり身を伏せて
6 **in cover you wouldn't think would hide a hare** ウサギさえ隠れられそうにない（と思うような）ところに（you は一般人称）
7 **can't very well send** 送り込むわけにはいかない　**that sort of a show** そういう場面に（ライオンが飛びかかってくる場面）
8 **bound to get mauled** きっと襲われる
10 **shauri** シャウリ（スワヒリ語で「役割」）　11 **signed** 契約している
13 **It was out** 口から言葉が出た　14 **before he knew he'd said it** 自分で気づくより先に
16 **as an afterthought** 思い直して　18 **pitiful look** みじめな表情
19 **That's what I'm hired for** そのためにわたしが雇われている
24 **occupation** 関心事　25 **problem he presented** ライオンが引き起こした問題　26 **note** 認識する　27 **windy** 臆病な

"What do you mean?"

"Why not just leave him?"

"You mean pretend to ourselves he hasn't been hit?"

"No. Just drop it."

"It isn't done."

"Why not?"

"For one thing, he's certain to be suffering. For another, some one else might run onto him."

"I see."

"But you don't have to have anything to do with it."

"I'd like to," Macomber said. "I'm just scared, you know."

"I'll go ahead when we go in," Wilson said, "with Kongoni tracking. You keep behind me and a little to one side. Chances are we'll hear him growl. If we see him we'll both shoot. Don't worry about anything. I'll keep you backed up. As a matter of fact, you know, perhaps you'd better not go. It might be much better. Why don't you go over and join the Memsahib while I just get it over with?"

"No, I want to go."

"All right," said Wilson. "But don't go in if you don't want to. This is my *shauri* now, you know."

"I want to go," said Macomber.

They sat under a tree and smoked.

"Want to go back and speak to the Memsahib while we're waiting?" Wilson asked.

"No."

"I'll just step back and tell her to be patient."

3 **pretend to ourselves he hasn't been hit** ライオンに弾が当たっていないふりをする
4 **drop it** なかったことにする
5 **It isn't done** それはだめだ
8 **run onto him** ライオンに出くわす
10 **have anything to do** 何かする
13 **with Kongoni tracking** コンゴニ（銃器係の名）についてこさせる 14 **to one side** 片側に 17 **keep you backed up**（コンゴニに）あなたを援護させる 20 **get it over with** 片づける
29 **patient** がまんして待つ

"Good," said Macomber. He sat there, sweating under his arms, his mouth dry, his stomach hollow feeling, wanting to find courage to tell Wilson to go on and finish off the lion without him. He could not know that Wilson was furious because he had not noticed the state he was in earlier and sent him back to his wife. While he sat there Wilson came up. "I have your big gun," he said. "Take it. We've given him time, I think. Come on."

Macomber took the big gun and Wilson said:

"Keep behind me and about five yards to the right and do exactly as I tell you." Then he spoke in Swahili to the two gun-bearers who looked the picture of gloom.

"Let's go," he said.

"Could I have a drink of water?" Macomber asked. Wilson spoke to the older gun-bearer, who wore a canteen on his belt, and the man unbuckled it, unscrewed the top and handed it to Macomber, who took it noticing how heavy it seemed and how hairy and shoddy the felt covering was in his hand. He raised it to drink and looked ahead at the high grass with the flat-topped trees behind it. A breeze was blowing toward them and the grass rippled gently in the wind. He looked at the gun-bearer and he could see the gun-bearer was suffering too with fear.

Thirty-five yards into the grass the big lion lay flattened out along the ground. His ears were back and his only movement was a slight twitching up and down of his long, black-tufted tail. He had turned at bay as soon as he had reached this cover and he was sick with the

₃ **finish off** とどめを刺す ₅ **he had not noticed** マカンバーが気づかなかった **the state he was in earlier** 自分がさっきどんな状況にあったか

₁₂ **picture of** 〜を絵に描いたような

₁₅ **canteen** 水筒 ₁₆ **unbuckled** バックルをはずした ₁₈ **hairy** 毛が生えたような **shoddy** ざらついている ₁₉ **felt covering** フェルト地のカバー ₂₀ **flat-topped trees** 上部が平たい木々 ₂₂ **rippled** 波打っていた ₂₃ **suffering** おびえている

₂₅ **flattened out** ぺったり身を伏せている ₂₆ **back** 倒れている ₂₇ **twitching** ひくひく動く ₂₈ **black-tufted** 黒い房になった **turned** 反撃する気でいた **at bay** 追いつめられて

wound through his full belly, and weakening with the wound through his lungs that brought a thin foamy red to his mouth each time he breathed. His flanks were wet and hot and flies were on the little openings the solid bullets had made in his tawny hide, and his big yellow eyes, narrowed with hate, looked straight ahead, only blinking when the pain came as he breathed, and his claws dug in the soft baked earth. All of him, pain, sickness, hatred and all of his remaining strength, was tightening into an absolute concentration for a rush. He could hear the men talking and he waited, gathering all of himself into this preparation for a charge as soon as the men would come into the grass. As he heard their voices his tail stiffened to twitch up and down, and, as they came into the edge of the grass, he made a coughing grunt and charged.

Kongoni, the old gun-bearer, in the lead watching the blood spoor, Wilson watching the grass for any movement, his big gun ready, the second gun-bearer looking ahead and listening, Macomber close to Wilson, his rifle cocked, they had just moved into the grass when Macomber heard the blood-choked coughing grunt, and saw the swishing rush in the grass. The next thing he knew he was running; running wildly, in panic in the open, running toward the stream.

He heard the *ca-ra-wong!* of Wilson's big rifle, and again in a second crashing *carawong!* and turning saw the lion, horrible-looking now, with half his head seeming to be gone, crawling toward Wilson in the edge of

1 **full belly** 大きな腹   2 **lungs** 肺 **brought thin foamy red to his mouth** 薄い泡まじりの血を口に運んだ   3 **flanks** 横腹   4 **flies** ハエ   5 **tawny hide** 黄褐色の皮   7 **blinking** まばたきする   8 **baked** 日光で焼けた   10 **tightening into** かたまって〜になる   **rush** 襲いかかること   14 **stiffened** こわばった   **twitch up and down** 上下にヒクヒク動く   16 **grunt** うなり声   21 **cocked** 撃鉄を起こした状態にある   22 **blood-choked** 血がのどに詰まった   23 **swishing** ヒューッと音を立てるような   26 **ca-ra-wong!** ウィルソンの銃の音   27 **turning** 振り返りながら

the tall grass while the red-faced man worked the bolt on the short ugly rifle and aimed carefully as another blasting *carawong!* came from the muzzle, and the crawling, heavy, yellow bulk of the lion stiffened and the huge, mutilated head slid forward and Macomber, standing by himself in the clearing where he had run, holding a loaded rifle, while two black men and a white man looked back at him in contempt, knew the lion was dead. He came toward Wilson, his tallness all seeming a naked reproach, and Wilson looked at him and said:

"Want to take pictures?"

"No," he said.

That was all any one had said until they reached the motor car. Then Wilson had said:

"Hell of a fine lion. Boys will skin him out. We might as well stay here in the shade."

Macomber's wife had not looked at him nor he at her and he had sat by her in the back seat with Wilson sitting in the front seat. Once he had reached over and taken his wife's hand without looking at her and she had removed her hand from his. Looking across the stream to where the gun-bearers were skinning out the lion he could see that she had been able to see the whole thing. While they sat there his wife had reached forward and put her hand on Wilson's shoulder. He turned and she had leaned forward over the low seat and kissed him on the mouth.

"Oh, I say," said Wilson, going redder than his natural baked color.

1 **red faced man** ウィルスンのこと　**bolt** ボルトハンドル
3 **blasting** 爆発音　**muzzle** 銃口　4 **crawling** 這うように動いている　**bulk** ライオンの体　5 **mutilated head** 頭の一部を失った　6 **clearing** 空き地　7 **loaded** 弾丸をこめてある　8 **in contempt** 軽蔑の目で　**knew** 主語はマカンバー　9 **his tallness** マカンバーの背の高さ　**seeming** 〜のようにみえる　10 **naked reproach** むき出しの非難
15 **Hell of** ものすごく　**skin him out** ライオンの皮をはぐ　**might as well** 〜したほうがいい
17 **nor he at her** マカンバーのほうも妻に目を向けなかった
28 **I say** おやおや　**going redder** 赤い顔をさらに赤くして

"Mr. Robert Wilson," she said. "The beautiful red-faced Mr. Robert Wilson."

Then she sat down beside Macomber again and looked away across the stream to where the lion lay, with uplifted, white-muscled, tendon-marked naked forearms, and white bloating belly, as the black men fleshed away the skin. Finally the gun-bearers brought the skin over, wet and heavy, and climbed in behind with it, rolling it up before they got in, and the motor car started. No one had said anything more until they were back in camp.

That was the story of the lion. Macomber did not know how the lion had felt before he started his rush, nor during it when the unbelievable smash of the .505 with a muzzle velocity of two tons had hit him in the mouth, nor what kept him coming after that, when the second ripping crash had smashed his hind quarters and he had come crawling on toward the crashing, blasting thing that had destroyed him. Wilson knew something about it and only expressed it by saying, "Damned fine lion," but Macomber did not know how Wilson felt about things either. He did not know how his wife felt except that she was through with him.

His wife had been through with him before but it never lasted. He was very wealthy, and would be much wealthier, and he knew she would not leave him ever now. That was one of the few things that he really knew. He knew about that, about motor cycles——that was earliest——about motor cars, about duck-shooting,

₅ **uplifted** 上向きになった **tendon-marked** 腱が見える ₆ **bloating** ふくらんでいる ₇ **fleshed away** はぎとった皮から肉をそぎ落とした **brought the skin over** 皮をもって車にもどってきた

₁₄ **smash** 一撃 ₁₅ **muzzle velocity** 銃口初速（破壊力を示す） **two tons** 2トンの（すさまじい） ₁₆ **what kept him coming after that** その後もライオンが突進を続けた理由 ₁₇ **ripping** 肉を切り裂いた **hind quarters** 後ろ半身 ₁₈ **blasting** 轟音を立てる ₂₃ **she was through with him** 彼女がマカンバーに愛想をつかした

₂₄ **had been through with him before** 過去にも愛想をつかしたことがあった **it never lasted** その状態は決して続かなかった ₂₅ **wealthy** 裕福な **would be much wealthier** 今後さらに裕福になるだろう ₂₈ **motor cycles** オートバイ **that was earliest** それは最初に（若いころに）知った事柄だ ₂₉ **duck-shooting** カモ撃ち

about fishing, trout, salmon and big-sea, about sex in books, many books, too many books, about all court games, about dogs, not much about horses, about hanging on to his money, about most of the other things his world dealt in, and about his wife not leaving him. His wife had been a great beauty and she was still a great beauty in Africa, but she was not a great enough beauty any more at home to be able to leave him and better herself and she knew it and he knew it. She had missed the chance to leave him and he knew it. If he had been better with women she would probably have started to worry about him getting another new, beautiful wife; but she knew too much about him to worry about him either. Also, he had always had a great tolerance which seemed the nicest thing about him if it were not the most sinister.

All in all they were known as a comparatively happily married couple, one of those whose disruption is often rumored but never occurs, and as the society columnist put it, they were adding more than a spice of *adventure* to their much envied and ever-enduring *Romance* by a *Safari* in what was known as *Darkest Africa* until the Martin Johnsons lighted it on so many silver screens where they were pursuing *Old Simba* the lion, the buffalo, *Tembo* the elephant and as well collecting specimens for the Museum of Natural History. This same columnist had reported them *on the verge* at least three times in the past and they had been. But they always made it up. They had a sound basis of union. Margot was too

1 **big-sea** 海の大きな獲物　**sex in books** 本の中で描かれるセックス　2 **court games** コートを使う球技　3 **hanging on to his money** 財産を維持すること　5 **dealt in** 関連する　8 **at home** 祖国（アメリカ）では　**better herself** 今より裕福な暮らしをする　11 **better with women** もっと女に慣れていたら　15 **if it were not the most sinister** もしこれほど陰険でなければ

17 **All in all** 概して　18 **disruption** 破局　19 **society columnist** 社交界のゴシップ記事を書く人　20 **put it** 記事に書いた　**a spice of adventure** 冒険というスパイス　21 **ever-enduring Romance** 永遠に終わることのないロマンス　**by a Safari** サファリに行くことによって　22 **Darkest Africa** 暗黒のアフリカ（謎の多い奥地をこう呼んでいた）　23 **Martin Johnsons** アフリカの自然を撮影したドキュメンタリー映画作家（1884~1937）とその妻　**lighted it** 映し出した　**silver screens** 映画のスクリーン　24 **Old Simba** ドキュメンタリー映画で追跡撮影したライオンの名　25 **Tembo** 映画で追跡撮影したゾウの名　**specimens** 標本　27 **on the verge** 破局寸前だ　28 **they had been** 実際そのとおりだった　**made it up** 仲直りをする　29 **sound** 安定した

beautiful for Macomber to divorce her and Macomber had too much money for Margot ever to leave him.

It was now about three o'clock in the morning and Francis Macomber, who had been asleep a little while after he had stopped thinking about the lion, wakened and then slept again, woke suddenly, frightened in a dream of the bloody-headed lion standing over him, and listening while his heart pounded, he realized that his wife was not in the other cot in the tent. He lay awake with that knowledge for two hours.

At the end of that time his wife came into the tent, lifted her mosquito bar and crawled cozily into bed.

"Where have you been?" Macomber asked in the darkness.

"Hello," she said. "Are you awake?"

"Where have you been?"

"I just went out to get a breath of air."

"You did, like hell."

"What do you want me to say, darling?"

"Where have you been?"

"Out to get a breath of air."

"That's a new name for it. You *are* a bitch."

"Well, you're a coward."

"All right," he said. "What of it?"

"Nothing as far as I'm concerned. But please let's not talk, darling, because I'm very sleepy."

"You think that I'll take anything."

"I know you will, sweet."

"Well, I won't."

8 **listening**（どきどきしながら）耳を澄ませている　10 **with that knowledge** そのことに気づきながら
12 **cozily** 心地よさそうに
18 **You did, like hell** ああ、そうだろうね（相手の言葉を肯定する表現を使いながら、逆に否定する皮肉）
22 **a new name for it** 新しい言いわけ　**a bitch** 売女
27 **take anything** なんでも許す

"Please, darling, let's not talk. I'm so very sleepy."

"There wasn't going to be any of that. You promised there wouldn't be."

"Well, there is now," she said sweetly.

"You said if we made this trip that there would be none of that. You promised."

"Yes, darling. That's the way I meant it to be. But the trip was spoiled yesterday. We don't have to talk about it, do we?"

"You don't wait long when you have an advantage, do you?"

"Please let's not talk. I'm so sleepy, darling."

"I'm going to talk."

"Don't mind me then, because I'm going to sleep." And she did.

At breakfast they were all three at the table before daylight and Francis Macomber found that, of all the many men that he had hated, he hated Robert Wilson the most.

"Sleep well?" Wilson asked in his throaty voice, filling a pipe.

"Did you?"

"Topping," the white hunter told him.

You bastard, thought Macomber, you insolent bastard.

So she woke him when she came in, Wilson thought, looking at them both with his flat, cold eyes. Well, why doesn't he keep his wife where she belongs? What does he think I am, a bloody plaster saint? Let him keep her where she belongs. It's his own fault.

2 **There wasn't going to be any of that** そういうこと（妻の浮気）は起こらないはずだった　**promised there wouldn't be** もうしないと約束した
4 **there is now** 今起こっている（浮気を認めている）
5 **there would be none of that** そういうことは絶対にしない
7 **That's the way I meant it to be** あのときはそのつもりだった
8 **spoiled** 台無しになった
10 **have an advantage** 優位に立つ
20 **throaty** しわがれた　**filling a pipe** パイプに煙草の葉を詰めながら
23 **Topping** すばらしくよく眠れた
24 **You bastard** この野郎　**insolent** 横柄な
25 **So** この様子からすると　26 **flat** 無表情な　27 **where she belongs** 彼女のいるべき場所（自分のそば）　28 **bloody** とんでもない　**plaster saint** 非の打ち所がない人

"Do you think we'll find buffalo?" Margot asked, pushing away a dish of apricots.

"Chance of it," Wilson said and smiled at her. "Why don't you stay in camp?"

"Not for anything," she told him.

"Why not order her to stay in camp?" Wilson said to Macomber.

"You order her," said Macomber coldly.

"Let's not have any ordering, nor," turning to Macomber, "any silliness, Francis," Margot said quite pleasantly.

"Are you ready to start?" Macomber asked.

"Any time," Wilson told him. "Do you want the Memsahib to go?"

"Does it make any difference whether I do or not?"

The hell with it, thought Robert Wilson. The utter complete hell with it. So this is what it's going to be like. Well, this is what it's going to be like, then.

"Makes no difference," he said.

"You're sure you wouldn't like to stay in camp with her yourself and let me go out and hunt the buffalo?" Macomber asked.

"Can't do that," said Wilson. "Wouldn't talk rot if I were you."

"I'm not talking rot. I'm disgusted."

"Bad word, disgusted."

"Francis, will you please try to speak sensibly," his wife said.

"I speak too damned sensibly," Macomber said. "Did

5 **Not for anything** 絶対にいや
9 **Let's not have any ordering** 命令なんてやめましょうよ
10 **any silliness** 愚かしい態度もやめてちょうだい（夫のウィルスンへの態度を指している）
16 **The hell with it** どうなろうと構わない　**utter complete** まったくの　17 **this is what it's going to be like** 結局こういうことになる
23 **talk rot** ばかげたことを言う
25 **disgusted** うんざりしている
27 **sensibly** 分別をもって

you ever eat such filthy food?"

"Something wrong with the food?" asked Wilson quietly.

"No more than with everything else."

"I'd pull yourself together, laddybuck," Wilson said very quietly. "There's a boy waits at table that understands a little English."

"The hell with him."

Wilson stood up and puffing on his pipe strolled away, speaking a few words in Swahili to one of the gun-bearers who was standing waiting for him. Macomber and his wife sat on at the table. He was staring at his coffee cup.

"If you make a scene I'll leave you, darling," Margot said quietly.

"No, you won't."

"You can try it and see."

"You won't leave me."

"No," she said. "I won't leave you and you'll behave yourself."

"Behave myself? That's a way to talk. Behave myself."

"Yes. Behave yourself."

"Why don't *you* try behaving?"

"I've tried it so long. So very long."

"I hate that red-faced swine," Macomber said. "I loathe the sight of him."

"He's really *very* nice."

"Oh, *shut up,*" Macomber almost shouted. Just then

1 **filthy** 不潔な
5 **pull yourself together** 自制心をとりもどす　**laddybuck** ガキめ（侮蔑的な呼びかけ）　6 **waits at table** 給仕をする
9 **strolled away** 歩き去った
14 **make a scene** みっともないまねをする
19 **behave yourself** 行儀よくする
21 **That's a way to talk** ずいぶんな言い方だな
24 **Why don't you try behaving?** おまえのほうこそ（強調）行儀よくしたらどうだ？
26 **swine** ブタ（卑劣な野郎）　27 **loathe the sight** 見るのもいやだ

the car came up and stopped in front of the dining tent and the driver and the two gun-bearers got out. Wilson walked over and looked at the husband and wife sitting there at the table.

"Going shooting?" he asked.

"Yes," said Macomber, standing up. "Yes."

"Better bring a woolly. It will be cool in the car," Wilson said.

"I'll get my leather jacket," Margot said.

"The boy has it," Wilson told her. He climbed into the front with the driver and Francis Macomber and his wife sat, not speaking, in the back seat.

Hope the silly beggar doesn't take a notion to blow the back of my head off, Wilson thought to himself. Women *are* a nuisance on safari.

The car was grinding down to cross the river at a pebbly ford in the gray daylight and then climbed, angling up the steep bank, where Wilson had ordered a way shovelled out the day before so they could reach the parklike wooded rolling country on the far side.

It was a good morning, Wilson thought. There was a heavy dew and as the wheels went through the grass and low bushes he could smell the odor of the crushed fronds. It was an odor like verbena and he liked this early morning smell of the dew, the crushed bracken and the look of the tree trunks showing black through the early morning mist, as the car made its way through the untracked, parklike country. He had put the two in the back seat out of his mind now and was thinking about

7 **woolly** セーター
13 **Hope** 〜だといいが　**the silly beggar** この愚か者　**take a notion** いきなり〜しようと思い立つ　**blow 〜 off** を吹っ飛ばす
15 **Women are** 女というものは　**nuisance** やっかい者
16 **grinding** 音を立てて進む　**pebbly ford** 石だらけの浅瀬
17 **angling up** ななめにのぼっていく　19 **shovelled out** シャベルで道を開く　20 **wooded rolling country** 木々の生えたなだらかな起伏のある原野　**on the far side** 川の対岸の
23 **crushed fronds** タイヤでつぶされた葉　24 **verbena** バーベナ（クマツヅラ属のハーブ）　25 **bracken** シダ類　26 **trunks** 幹　28 **untracked** 道が作られていない　**the two** マカンバー夫妻　29 **out of his mind** 頭から締めだす

buffalo. The buffalo that he was after stayed in the daytime in a thick swamp where it was impossible to get a shot, but in the night they fed out into an open stretch of country and if he could come between them and their swamp with the car, Macomber would have a good chance at them in the open. He did not want to hunt buff with Macomber in thick cover. He did not want to hunt buff or anything else with Macomber at all, but he was a professional hunter and he had hunted with some rare ones in his time. If they got buff today there would only be rhino to come and the poor man would have gone through his dangerous game and things might pick up. He'd have nothing more to do with the woman and Macomber would get over that too. He must have gone through plenty of that before by the look of things. Poor beggar. He must have a way of getting over it. Well, it was the poor sod's own bloody fault.

He, Robert Wilson, carried a double size cot on safari to accommodate any windfalls he might receive. He had hunted for a certain clientele, the international, fast, sporting set, where the women did not feel they were getting their money's worth unless they had shared that cot with the white hunter. He despised them when he was away from them although he liked some of them well enough at the time, but he made his living by them; and their standards were his standards as long as they were hiring him.

They were his standards in all except the shooting. He had his own standards about the killing and they could

2 **thick swamp** ぬかるんだ湿地 3 **open stretch** 開けた場所
4 **between them and their swamp** バッファローと湿地の間
7 **buff** バッファロー　**thick cover** 生い茂った下生え　10 **rare ones** 変人たち　**in his time** ガイドとしてのキャリアにおいて
would only be rhino to come そうすれば、あとはサイくらいしか狩るものはない　11 **the poor man** 哀れな男（マカンバー）
12 **through his dangerous game** 危険なゲーム（狩り）を終えて　**pick up** いい方向に向かう　14 **get over that** 妻の浮気を克服する　15 **plenty of that** 度重なる浮気　**by the look of things** ふたりの様子を見たところでは　17 **the poor sod's** この哀れなやつの

18 **cot** 簡易ベッド　19 **accommodate** 泊める　**windfalls** 思いがけない授かり物　20 **clientele** 顧客　**fast** ふしだらな
21 **sporting set** 危険を好む連中　22 **getting their money's worth** 払った金に相応のサービスを受ける　23 **despised** 軽蔑した　25 **at the time** ガイドをしている間は　**he made his living by them** そういう連中とのつきあいで生計を立てていた
28 **They were his standards in all** すべてにおいて客がウィルスンの価値基準だった　29 **they could live up to them** 客が彼の価値基準に従えばいい

live up to them or get someone else to hunt them. He knew, too, that they all respected him for this. This Macomber was an odd one though. Damned if he wasn't. Now the wife. Well, the wife. Yes, the wife. Hm, the wife. Well he'd dropped all that. He looked around at them. Macomber sat grim and furious. Margot smiled at him. She looked younger today, more innocent and fresher and not so professionally beautiful. What's in her heart God knows, Wilson thought. She hadn't talked much last night. At that it was a pleasure to see her.

The motor car climbed up a slight rise and went on through the trees and then out into a grassy prairie-like opening and kept in the shelter of the trees along the edge, the driver going slowly and Wilson looking carefully out across the prairie and all along its far side. He stopped the car and studied the opening with his field glasses. Then he motioned to the driver to go on and the car moved slowly along, the driver avoiding warthog holes and driving around the mud castles ants had built. Then, looking across the opening, Wilson suddenly turned and said,

"By God, there they are!"

And looking where he pointed, while the car jumped forward and Wilson spoke in rapid Swahili to the driver, Macomber saw three huge, black animals looking almost cylindrical in their long heaviness, like big black tank cars, moving at a gallop across the far edge of the open prairie. They moved at a stiff-necked, stiff bodied gallop and he could see the upswept wide black horns

3 **odd** 変わっている　**Damned if he wasn't** ものすごく変わっている　4 **Hm** ふうむ（考えこんでいる様子）　5 **dropped** 水に流す　**all that** 昨夜のすべて　6 **them** マカンバー夫妻　**grim** 不機嫌そうな　8 **professionally** 玄人じみた　10 **At that** それにもかかわらず

12 **prairie-like** 草原のような　14 **edge** 草原の端　15 **all along its far side** 草原のはるか彼方を（眺めわたす）　16 **field glasses** 双眼鏡　17 **motioned** 合図する　18 **warthog** イボイノシシ　19 **mud castles** アリ塚　21 **turned** 振り返った

26 **cylindrical** 円筒形の　**long heaviness** 長く重そうな体　27 **tank cars** タンクローリー車　28 **a stiff-necked** 首を硬くして　**stiff bodied gallop** 体が固まったような走り方　29 **upswept** 上向きにカーブした

on their heads as they galloped heads out; the heads not moving.

"They're three old bulls," Wilson said. "We'll cut them off before they get to the swamp."

The car was going a wild forty-five miles an hour across the open and as Macomber watched, the buffalo got bigger and bigger until he could see the gray, hairless, scabby look of one huge bull and how his neck was a part of his shoulders and the shiny black of his horns as he galloped a little behind the others that were strung out in that steady plunging gait; and then, the car swaying as though it had just jumped a road, they drew up close and he could see the plunging hugeness of the bull, and the dust in his sparsely haired hide, the wide boss of horn and his outstretched, wide-nostrilled muzzle, and he was raising his rifle when Wilson shouted, "Not from the car, you fool!" and he had no fear, only hatred of Wilson, while the brakes clamped on and the car skidded, plowing sideways to an almost stop and Wilson was out on one side and he on the other, stumbling as his feet hit the still speeding-by of the earth, and then he was shooting at the bull as he moved away, hearing the bullets whunk into him, emptying his rifle at him as he moved steadily away, finally remembering to get his shots forward into the shoulder, and as he fumbled to re-load, he saw the bull was down. Down on his knees, his big head tossing, and seeing the other two still galloping he shot at the leader and hit him. He shot again and missed and he heard the *carawonging* roar as

1 heads out 頭を前に突き出して
3 old bulls バッファローの成牛　cut them off 湿地に入るのを阻止する
5 a wild forty-five miles an hour 時速70キロの猛スピードで
8 scabby（かさぶたなどで）荒れて汚らしい　9 shiny black 黒光りする　11 strung out 一列に並んで　steady plunging gait 安定した高速での突進　12 swaying 揺れる　drew up close バッファローに近づく　13 plunging 突進する　hugeness 巨体（最後尾のバッファロー）　14 dust 土の汚れ　sparsely haired hide 毛のまばらな皮　the wide boss 大きく広がった突起　15 outstretched 前に突き出した　wide-nostrilled 鼻孔が横に広い　muzzle 鼻面　17 fool 馬鹿者　18 brakes ブレーキ　clamped on かけられた　19 skidded 横すべりした　plowing 土をはねあげながら　20 stumbling よろめいて　21 still speeding-by of the earth まだ動いている地面（車が完全にはとまっていないため）　22 he moved away 主語はバッファロー　23 whunk（鈍い音を立てて）命中する　emptying his rifle 弾がなくなるまで撃ち続ける　24 as he moved steadily away 主語はバッファロー　finally remembering to ようやく〜するべきだと思い出して　26 fumbled to re-load おぼつかない手で弾をこめる　27 tossing 上に突き上げて　seeing 主語はマカンバー　29 carawonging ウィルソンの大口径の銃声

Wilson shot and saw the leading bull slide forward onto his nose.

"Get that other," Wilson said. "Now you're shooting!"

But the other bull was moving steadily at the same gallop and he missed, throwing a spout of dirt, and Wilson missed and the dust rose in a cloud and Wilson shouted, "Come on. He's too far!" and grabbed his arm and they were in the car again, Macomber and Wilson hanging on the sides and rocketing swayingly over the uneven ground, drawing up on the steady, plunging, heavy-necked, straight-moving gallop of the bull.

They were behind him and Macomber was filling his rifle, dropping shells onto the ground, jamming it, clearing the jam, then they were almost up with the bull when Wilson yelled "Stop," and the car skidded so that it almost swung over and Macomber fell forward onto his feet, slammed his bolt forward and fired as far forward as he could aim into the galloping, rounded black back, aimed and shot again, then again, then again, and the bullets, all of them hitting, had no effect on the buffalo that he could see. Then Wilson shot, the roar deafening him, and he could see the bull stagger. Macomber shot again, aiming carefully, and down he came, onto his knees.

"All right," Wilson said. "Nice work. That's the three."

Macomber felt a drunken elation.

"How many times did you shoot?" he asked.

1 **slide forward onto his nose** 前のめりになって鼻から倒れる
6 **throwing a spout of dirt** 土をまきあげながら 10 **hanging on the sides** (車の)左右にしがみついて **rocketing** 猛スピードで進む **swayingly** 揺れながら 11 **uneven** 凹凸のある **drawing up on** に迫っていく **steady** 安定した 12 **heavy-necked** 首が太い
14 **shells** 弾丸 **jamming** 弾が途中で詰まって 15 **clearing the jam** 詰まりをとる **almost up with the bull** バッファローにまもなく追いつく 17 **swung over** 横転する **fell forward onto his feet** 倒れるように飛びおりて着地した 18 **slammed** 強く押した **bolt** ボルトハンドル 19 **rounded black back** 黒く丸い背中 22 **deafening** 耳をつんざく 23 **stagger** よろめく
26 **That's the three** これで三頭しとめた
28 **drunken elation** 酒に酔ったように興奮する

"Just three," Wilson said. "You killed the first bull. The biggest one. I helped you finish the other two. Afraid they might have got into cover. You had them killed. I was just mopping up a little. You shot damn well."

"Let's go to the car," said Macomber. "I want a drink."

"Got to finish off' that buff first," Wilson told him. The buffalo was on his knees and he jerked his head furiously and bellowed in pig-eyed, roaring rage as they came toward him.

"Watch he doesn't get up," Wilson said. Then, "Get a little broadside and take him in the neck just behind the ear."

Macomber aimed carefully at the center of the huge, jerking, rage-driven neck and shot. At the shot the head dropped forward.

"That does it," said Wilson. "Got the spine. They're a hell of a looking thing, aren't they?"

"Let's get the drink," said Macomber. In his life he had never felt so good.

In the car Macomber's wife sat very white-faced. "You were marvellous, darling," she said to Macomber. "What a ride."

"Was it rough?" Wilson asked.

"It was frightful. I've never been more frightened in my life."

"Let's all have a drink," Macomber said.

"By all means," said Wilson. "Give it to the Mem-

3 **got into cover** 見通しの利かない場所に逃げこむ 4 **mopping up** 仕上げ
8 **Got to finish oft that buff** あのバッファローを片づけなくてはならない 9 **jerked** 振りあげた 10 **bellowed** うなった **pig-eyed** ブタのような目で **they** ウィルスンとマカンバー
12 **Get a little broadside** 少し横のほうから 13 **take him in the neck** バッファローの首を撃つ
16 **rage-driven** 激しく動いている
18 **That does it** それでいい **Got the spine** 脊椎に命中した **a hell of a looking thing** 相当みごとなもの
23 **What a ride** すごいドライブだった
25 **rough** 手荒な
29 **By all means** ぜひそうしよう

sahib." She drank the neat whisky from the flask and shuddered a little when she swallowed. She handed the flask to Macomber who handed it to Wilson.

"It was frightfully exciting," she said. "It's given me a dreadful headache. I didn't know you were allowed to shoot them from cars though."

"No one shot from cars," said Wilson coldly.

"I mean chase them from cars."

"Wouldn't ordinarily," Wilson said. "Seemed sporting enough to me though while we were doing it. Taking more chance driving that way across the plain full of holes and one thing and another than hunting on foot. Buffalo could have charged us each time we shot if he liked. Gave him every chance. Wouldn't mention it to any one though. It's illegal if that's what you mean." .

"It seemed very unfair to me," Margot said, "chasing those big helpless things in a motor car."

"Did it?" said Wilson.

"What would happen if they heard about it in Nairobi?"

"I'd lose my licence for one thing. Other unpleasantnesses," Wilson said, taking a drink from the flask. "I'd be out of business."

"Really?"

"Yes, really."

"Well," said Macomber, and he smiled for the first time all day. "Now she has something on you."

"You have such a pretty way of putting things, Francis," Margot Macomber said. Wilson looked at them

1 **neat** ストレートの　**flask** ウィスキーなどを入れる携帯用の金属容器。フラスク　2 **shuddered** 身ぶるいした
9 **Wouldn't ordinarily** ふつうはやらない（車で獲物を追うことはしない）　**sporting** スリルがある　10 **Taking more chance driving** 車で追うほうがチャンスが多い　11 **that way** あんなふうに　**the plain full of holes and one thing and another** 穴やさまざまな障害のある原野（だが）　14 **Wouldn't mention it** 他言しないことにしている（主語はウィルスン）　15 **if that's what you mean** あなたが言っているのがそういう意味なら
19 **they** ナイロビの警察
21 **for one thing** ひとつ例を挙げれば　23 **out of business** 失業する
27 **has something on you** きみの弱みをにぎっている
28 **You have such a pretty way of putting things** 本当にひどい言い方をするのね

both. If a four-letter man marries a five-letter woman, he was thinking, what number of letters would their children be? What he said was, "We lost a gun-bearer. Did you notice it?"

"My God, no," Macomber said.

"Here he comes," Wilson said. "He's all right. He must have fallen off when we left the first bull."

Approaching them was the middle-aged gun-bearer, limping along in his knitted cap, khaki tunic, shorts and rubber sandals, gloomy-faced and disgusted looking. As he came up he called out to Wilson in Swahili and they all saw the change in the white hunter's face.

"What does he say?" asked Margot.

"He says the first bull got up and went into the bush," Wilson said with no expression in his voice.

"Oh," said Macomber blankly.

"Then it's going to be just like the lion," said Margot, full of anticipation.

"It's not going to be a damned bit like the lion," Wilson told her. "Did you want another drink, Macomber?"

"Thanks, yes," Macomber said. He expected the feeling he had had about the lion to come back but it did not. For the first time in his life he really felt wholly without fear. Instead of fear he had a feeling of definite elation. "We'll go and have a look at the second bull," Wilson said. "I'll tell the driver to put the car in the shade."

"What are you going to do?" asked Margaret Macomber.

1 **four-letter** 卑劣な（fuck や damn など四文字の汚い言葉が多いことから）　**five-letter** 前の four-letter を上回るほど卑劣な
2 **what number of letters** どれほど卑劣な
7 **fallen off** 車から落ちた　**left**（最初にしとめたバッファローを）放置した
9 **limping** 足を引きずりながら　**khaki tunic** カーキ色の上着
10 **disgusted looking** うんざりした表情
16 **blankly** 無表情で
17 **it's going to be just like the lion** これからライオンのときと同じことが起きる
19 **a damned bit** 少しも〜ない（否定の強調）
23 **wholly without** まったくない　24 **definite elation** 明らかな興奮

"Take a look at the buff," Wilson said.

"I'll come."

"Come along."

The three of them walked over to where the second buffalo bulked blackly in the open, head forward on the grass, the massive horns swung wide.

"He's a very good head," Wilson said. "That's close to a fifty-inch spread."

Macomber was looking at him with delight.

"He's hateful looking," said Margot. "Can't we go into the shade?"

"Of course," Wilson said. "Look," he said to Macomber, and pointed. "See that patch of bush?"

"Yes."

"That's where the first bull went in. The gun-bearer said when he fell off the bull was down. He was watching us helling along and the other two buff galloping. When he looked up there was the bull up and looking at him. Gun-bearer ran like hell and the bull went off slowly into that bush."

"Can we go in after him now?" asked Macomber eagerly.

Wilson looked at him appraisingly. Damned if this isn't a strange one, he thought. Yesterday he's scared sick and today he's a ruddy fire eater.

"No, we'll give him a while."

"Let's please go into the shade," Margot said. Her face was white and she looked ill.

They made their way to the car where it stood under a

1 **take a look at the buff** バッファローの様子を見にいく
5 **bulked blackly** 黒い巨体があった 6 **swung wide** 大きく広がっていた
8 **a fifty inch spread** 角から角まで、角を入れて約 1.3 メートル
9 **him** バッファロー
10 **hateful looking** 恨みがましい表情
13 **that patch of bush** 茂みの一帯
16 **fell off** 自分が車から落ちた **down** 倒れている 17 **helling along** 猛スピードで進む 18 **up** 立ち上がっている 19 **like hell** 必死に
23 **appraisingly** 感心したように **Damned if this isn't a strange one** こいつは相当な変わり者だ 24 **scared sick** 恐怖で青ざめていた 25 **ruddy** 血色のいい **fire eater** 怖いもの知らず
26 **give him a while** しばらく放っておく
29 **made their way to** 〜のところへ行く

single, widespreading tree and all climbed in.

"Chances are he's dead in there," Wilson remarked. "After a little we'll have a look."

Macomber felt a wild unreasonable happiness that he had never known before.

"By God, that was a chase," he said. "I've never felt any such feeling. Wasn't it marvellous, Margot?"

"I hated it."

"Why?"

"I hated it," she said bitterly. "I loathed it."

"You know I don't think I'd ever be afraid of anything again," Macomber said to Wilson. "Something happened in me after we first saw the buff and started after him. Like a dam bursting. It was pure excitement."

"Cleans out your liver," said Wilson. "Damn funny things happen to people."

Macomber's face was shining. "You know something did happen to me," he said. "I feel absolutely different."

His wife said nothing and eyed him strangely. She was sitting far back in the seat and Macomber was sitting forward talking to Wilson who turned sideways talking over the back of the front seat.

"You know, I'd like to try another lion," Macomber said. "I'm really not afraid of them now. After all, what can they do to you?"

"That's it," said Wilson. "Worst one can do is kill you. How does it go? Shakespeare. Damned good. See if I can remember. Oh, damned good. Used to quote it to myself at one time. Let's see. 'By my troth, I care not;

2 **Chances are** おそらく〜だろう　**remarked** 言った
4 **unreasonable** 理性を欠いた　**he had never known before** 今まで経験したことのない
6 **that was a chase** すごい追跡だった
10 **loathed** いやでたまらなかった
14 **dam bursting** ダムが決壊する
15 **Cleans out your liver** (興奮が)肝をきれいにしてくれる
19 **eyed him strangely** 奇妙なものを見るような目で見た
20 **far back** 後ろにもたれて　21 **turned sideways** 横を向いて
22 **the back of the front seat** 前の席の背もたれ
24 **what can they do to you?** ライオンになにができるというんだ？(you は一般人称)
26 **That's it** そのとおりだ　**Worst one can do** ライオンにできる最悪のこと　27 **How does it go?** どんな科白だったっけ？ **Shakespeare** シェイクスピアの言葉だ　**Damned good** ものすごくいい　**See if I can remember** 思い出せるかな　28 **Used to** 昔は〜したものだ　**quote it to myself** 暗唱する　29 **at one time** 一時期は　**By my troth** わたしは誓う(「ヘンリー四世」第2部3幕2場からの引用)　**care not** (=don't care)

a man can die but once; we owe God a death and let it go which way it will, he that dies this year is quit for the next.' Damned fine, eh?"

He was very embarrassed, having brought out this thing he had lived by, but he had seen men come of age before and it always moved him. It was not a matter of their twenty-first birthday.

It had taken a strange chance of hunting, a sudden precipitation into action without opportunity for worrying beforehand, to bring this about with Macomber, but regardless of how it had happened it had most certainly happened. Look at the beggar now, Wilson thought. It's that some of them stay little boys so long, Wilson thought. Sometimes all their lives. Their figures stay boyish when they're fifty. The great American boy-men. Damned strange people. But he liked this Macomber now. Damned strange fellow. Probably meant the end of cuckoldry too. Well, that would be a damned good thing. Damned good thing. Beggar had probably been afraid all his life. Don't know what started it. But over now. Hadn't had time to be afraid with the buff. That and being angry too. Motor car too. Motor cars made it familiar. Be a damn fire eater now. He'd seen it in the war work the same way. More of a change than any loss of virginity. Fear gone like an operation. Something else grew in its place. Main thing a man had. Made him into a man. Women knew it too. No bloody fear.

From the far corner of the seat Margaret Macomber looked at the two of them. There was no change in Wil-

1 we owe God a death われわれは神から死を授かる　let it go which way it will なりゆきにまかせればいい　2 quit for the next 来年は死を免れる

4 brought out this thing he had lived by 人生の信条としてきたものを話してしまった　5 come of age before 大人になる　6 it always moved him そういう場面ではいつも感動した　7 twenty-first birthday 二十一歳の誕生日（未熟なころを指す）　8 It to 以下を指す　had taken a strange chance of hunting 普通ではありえないハンティングという危険を冒すことが必要だった　9 precipitation into action いきなり行動せざるをえなくなった　10 to bring this about with Macomber（恐怖心を克服すること）をマカンバーにもたらした　11 regardless of how it had happened どういう経緯で起こったにせよ　13 It's that そういうものだ　stay little boys 幼い少年のままでいる　17 Probably meant the end of cuckoldry too たぶんこれでもう妻を寝とられることもないだろう　20 Don't know what started it 何が原因で始まったのかは知らない　over now もう終わった　21 Hadn't had time する時間がなかった。主語はマカンバー　That and being angry おまけに怒りを抱えていた　22 Motor car too 車の効果もあった　Motor cars made it familiar 車に乗ると気持ちが落ち着く　23 fire eater 怖いもの知らず　24 work the same way 同じ作用が起きる　loss of virginity 童貞の喪失　25 Fear gone 恐怖心が消えた　like an operation 手術で切除したように　26 Main thing a man had 男の中核となるもの　27 No bloody fear 恐怖心などなくなってしまうのだ

son. She saw Wilson as she had seen him the day before when she had first realized what his great talent was. But she saw the change in Francis Macomber now.

"Do you have that feeling of happiness about what's going to happen?" Macomber asked, still exploring his new wealth.

"You're not supposed to mention it," Wilson said, looking in the other's face. "Much more fashionable to say you're scared. Mind you, you'll be scared too, plenty of times."

"But you *have* a feeling of happiness about action to come?"

"Yes," said Wilson. "There's that. Doesn't do to talk too much about all this. Talk the whole thing away. No pleasure in anything if you mouth it up too much."

"You're both talking rot," said Margot. "Just because you've chased some helpless animals in a motor car you talk like heroes."

"Sorry," said Wilson. "I have been gassing too much." She's worried about it already, he thought.

"If you don't know what we're talking about why not keep out of it?" Macomber asked his wife.

"You've gotten awfully brave, awfully suddenly," his wife said contemptuously, but her contempt was not secure. She was very afraid of something.

Macomber laughed, a very natural hearty laugh. "You know I *have*," he said. "I really have."

"Isn't it sort of late?" Margot said bitterly. Because she had done the best she could for many years back

5 **his new wealth** 新たな富（自信のこと）
7 **You're not supposed to** 〜することは慎むべきだ　**mention it** そういうことを口に出して言う　8 **looking in the other's face** 相手の顔を見ながら　**fashionable** 流行の　9 **Mind you** いいか　10 **plenty of times** 何度も
11 **action to come** これから起きるできごと
13 **There's that** それはあるよ　**Doesn't do to talk** しゃべっても何の役にも立たない　14 **Talk the whole thing away** 話してしまうとなくなってしまう　15 **mouth it up too much** ぺらぺらしゃべりすぎる
16 **rot** くだらないこと
19 **gassing** 無駄話をする
21 **why not keep out of it?** 口をはさまないでくれ
24 **contempt** 蔑み　**secure** 確かなもの
27 **have** 勇敢になった（gotten brave が略されている）
28 **sort of** 少し　29 **for many years back** 今まで何年も

and the way they were together now was no one person's fault.

"Not for me," said Macomber.

Margot said nothing but sat back in the corner of the seat.

"Do you think we've given him time enough?" Macomber asked Wilson cheerfully.

"We might have a look," Wilson said. "Have you any solids left?"

"The gun-bearer has some."

Wilson called in Swahili and the older gun-bearer, who was skinning out one of the heads, straightened up, pulled a box of solids out of his pocket and brought them over to Macomber, who filled his magazine and put the remaining shells in his pocket.

"You might as well shoot the Springfield," Wilson said. "You're used to it. We'll leave the Mannlicher in the car with the Memsahib. Your gunbearer can carry your heavy gun. I've this damned cannon. Now let me tell you about them." He had saved this until the last because he did not want to worry Macomber. "When a buff comes he comes with his head high and thrust straight out. The boss of the horns covers any sort of a brain shot. The only shot is straight into the nose. The only other shot is into his chest or, if you're to one side, into the neck or the shoulders. After they've been hit once they take a hell of a lot of killing. Don't try anything fancy. Take the easiest shot there is. They've finished skinning out that head now. Should we get

1 **the way they were together now** 夫婦の今の状況　**no one person's fault** どちらか一方が原因というわけではない
3 **Not for me** 自分にとっては遅くない
8 **might have a look** 見てみるのもいいかもしれない　9 **solids left** 弾丸が残っている
14 **filled his magazine** 弾倉に弾をこめた　15 **shells** 弾丸
16 **Springfirld** スプリングフィールド銃　17 **Mannlicher** マンリッヒャー銃　19 **cannon** 大砲（大口径の銃のことを大げさにいっている）　23 **boss** 角の付け根の盛り上がっているところ　**covers** カバーする（頭を撃っても角の付け根のところではじかれてしまう）　25 **you're to one side** 横からなら　27 **hit once** 一度撃たれると　**a hell of** ものすごく　28 **fancy** 突飛なこと

started?"

He called to the gun-bearers, who came up wiping their hands, and the older one got into the back.

"I'll only take Kongoni," Wilson said. "The other can watch to keep the birds away."

As the car moved slowly across the open space toward the island of brushy trees that ran in a tongue of foliage along a dry water course that cut the open swale, Macomber felt his heart pounding and his mouth was dry again, but it was excitement, not fear.

"Here's where he went in," Wilson said. Then to the gun-bearer in Swahili, "Take the blood spoor."

The car was parallel to the patch of bush. Macomber, Wilson and the gun-bearer got down. Macomber, looking back, saw his wife, with the rifle by her side, looking at him. He waved to her and she did not wave back .

The brush was very thick ahead and the ground was dry. The middleaged gun-bearer was sweating heavily and Wilson had his hat down over his eyes and his red neck showed just ahead of Macomber. Suddenly the gun-bearer said something in Swahili to Wilson and ran forward.

"He's dead in there," Wilson said. "Good work," and he turned to grip Macomber's hand and as they shook hands, grinning at each other, the gun-bearer shouted wildly and they saw him coming out of the bush sideways, fast as a crab, and the bull coming, nose out, mouth tight closed, blood dripping, massive head straight out, coming in a charge, his little pig

3 **got into the back** 後部座席に乗りこんだ
5 **keep the birds away** 鳥が死骸にたからないようにする
7 **brushy trees** 枝葉の多い低木　**a tongue of foliage** 低木の緑が細長く伸びているもの　8 **swale** 低湿地
11 **where he went in** バッファローがやぶに入っていった場所
12 **blood spoor** 血の跡
13 **was parallel to** 〜と平行に
17 **brush** やぶ
24 **turned to grip** 手をにぎろうと振り返った　27 **sideways** 横向きで　**crab** カニ　28 **dripping** 滴らせながら　29 **in a charge** 突進して

eyes bloodshot as he looked at them. Wilson, who was ahead, was kneeling shooting, and Macomber, as he fired, unhearing his shot in the roaring of Wilson's gun, saw fragments like slate burst from the huge boss of the horns, and the head jerked, he shot again at the wide nostrils and saw the horns jolt again and fragments fly, and he did not see Wilson now and, aiming carefully, shot again with the buffalo's huge bulk almost on him and his rifle almost level with the on-coming head, nose out, and he could see the little wicked eyes and the head started to lower and he felt a sudden white-hot, blinding flash explode inside his head and that was all he ever felt.

Wilson had ducked to one side to get in a shoulder shot. Macomber had stood solid and shot for the nose, shooting a touch high each time and hitting the heavy horns, splintering and chipping them like hitting a slate roof, and Mrs. Macomber, in the car, had shot at the buffalo with the 6.5 Mannlicher as it seemed about to gore Macomber and had hit her husband about two inches up and a little to one side of the base of his skull.

Francis Macomber lay now, face down, not two yards from where the buffalo lay on his side and his wife knelt over him with Wilson beside her.

"I wouldn't turn him over," Wilson said.

The woman was crying hysterically.

"I'd get back in the car," Wilson said. "Where's the rifle?"

She shook her head, her face contorted. The gun-

1 **bloodshot** 血走っている　4 **fragments** かけら　**slate** 石板　5 **jerked** がくんと揺れる　6 **jolt** 揺れる　8 **bulk** 体　**almost on him** マカンバーの目の前に迫る　9 **level with** と同じ高さになる　11 **blinding** 目をくらませる

14 **ducked** よける　**to get in a shoulder shot** 肩を撃つために　16 **a touch high** 少し高い　17 **splintering** 砕く　**chipping** 削る　19 **6.5 Mannlicher** 6.5口径のマンリッヒャー銃　**gore** 角で突き刺す　20 **two inches up and a little to one side of the base of his skull** 夫の頭蓋骨の下から5センチで、少し片方に寄ったところ

25 **I wouldn't turn him over** おれなら遺体を仰向けにしたりしない（仮定法。しないほうがいいととめている）

29 **contorted** ゆがんでいる

bearer picked up the rifle.

"Leave it as it is," said Wilson. Then, "Go get Abdulla so that he may witness the manner of the accident."

He knelt down, took a handkerchief from his pocket, and spread it over Francis Macomber's crew-cropped head where it lay. The blood sank into the dry, loose earth.

Wilson stood up and saw the buffalo on his side, his legs out, his thinly-haired belly crawling with ticks. "Hell of a good bull," his brain registered automatically. "A good fifty inches, or better. Better." He called to the driver and told him to spread a blanket over the body and stay by it. Then he, walked over to the motor car where the woman sat crying in the corner.

"That was a pretty thing to do," he said in a toneless voice. "He *would* have left you too."

"Stop it," she said.

"Of course it's an accident," he said. "I know that."

"Stop it," she said.

"Don't worry," he said. "There will be a certain amount of unpleasantness but I will have some photographs taken that will be very useful at the inquest. There's the testimony of the gun-bearers and the driver too. You're perfectly all right."

"Stop it," she said.

"There's a hell of a lot to be done," he said. "And I'll have to send a truck off to the lake to wireless for a plane to take the three of us into Nairobi. Why didn't you poison him? That's what they do in England."

2 **Go get Abdulla** アブドゥラ（初出の人名）を呼んでこい
3 **manner of the accident** 事故の状況
5 **crew-cropped** 髪を短く刈った　6 **loose earth** もろい地面
9 **out** 投げ出して　**crawling with ticks** ダニがたかっている
10 **registered** 計算する　11 **A good fifty inches, or better** 優に120センチ以上
15 **That was a pretty thing to do** とんでもないことをしたもんだな　16 **He *would* have left you too**（仮定法）旦那の方も、もし生きていれば、あんたを置いて出て行ったでしょう
21 **have some photographs taken** 写真を撮らせておく
22 **inquest** 検死審問　23 **testimony** 証言　24 **perfectly all right** ぜったいに大丈夫
27 **to wireless** 無線で手配する　29 **poison** 毒をもる

"Stop it. Stop it. Stop it," the woman cried.

Wilson looked at her with his flat blue eyes.

"I'm through now," he said. "I was a little angry. I'd begun to like your husband."

"Oh, please stop it," she said. "Please stop it."

"That's better," Wilson said. "Please is much better. Now I'll stop."

2 **flat** 無表情な
3 **I'm through** 気分が鎮まった
6 **Please is much better** please をつけた命令文のほうがずっといい
7 **Now I'll stop** じゃあ、やめましょう

あとがき

　日本人が最も好きなアメリカ作家はおそらくヘミングウェイだろう。『武器よさらば』(1929年出版)『誰がために鐘は鳴る』(1940年出版)『老人と海』(1951年「ライフ」誌に掲載)など、どれもベストセラーになったことがあり、いまでも読み継がれているロングセラーだ。また、3作品ともに映画になったことがあり、日本でも公開されて評判になった。
　また短編集も愛読者が多い。その短編のなかでも最も有名で、最も読まれていて、最も愛されているのが「キリマンジャロの雪 (The Snows of Kilimanjaro)」だろう。
　まず、なにより冒頭の文章がすばらしい。

　キリマンジャロは雪におおわれた山で、標高19,710フィート、アフリカで最も高い山といわれている。その西の頂はマサイ語で「ンガイエ・ンガイ」と呼ばれている。「神の家」という意味だ。その西の頂近くに、ひからびて凍りついたヒョウの死骸がある。ヒョウがこんなに高いところまで何を求めてやってきたのかは、だれも知らない。

　こんな印象的な文章の後、アフリカにハンティングにきているハリーとヘレンの夫婦の物語が始まる。
　ハリーはふとしたけががもとで片脚が壊死しかけて

いる。簡易ベッドからあたりをながめて、死期が近いと思っている。近くをうろつくハイエナ、舞い降りるハゲワシ、腐っていく脚のにおい。ヘレンは、自分の死をほのめかすハリーをなだめ、励まし、元気づけようとする。ハリーは、ヘレンが止めるのもかまわずウィスキーを飲む。

そんな殺伐とした情景と、ぎくしゃくした夫婦の会話の合間に、ハリーの感情や、過去の回想がさしはさまれる。書く書くとつぶやきながら、結局、ひとつも作品を仕上げることができないまま死にかけている自分に対する忸怩たる思い、そんな自分を養ってくれているヘレンへの鬱屈した思い、それに第一次世界大戦のときの思い出が混じる。

ヘミングウェイというと、ボクシングをやったり、カリブ海でトローリングをやったり、アフリカでハンティングをやったりしている写真が有名で、いかにもアメリカのマッチョな男という印象が強いが、その作品に登場する男の多くは内向的で、どこか屈折していて、センチメンタルなところがある。人間としての、男ゆえの弱さをひしひしと感じさせる。

ここに収録したもう1編の「フランシス・マカンバーの短く幸せな生涯（The Short Happy Life of Francis Macomber）」も「キリマンジャロの雪」に似た設定の短編だ。アフリカにハンティングにきているアメリカ人夫婦が中心になっている。

マカンバーは襲いかかってくるライオンを撃ち損じるどころか、背を向けて逃げてしまう。そのライオン

を妻が見事に仕留める。その後、テントにもどって昼食をとるところから、この物語が始まる。

　マカンバーは心底、ライオンが恐ろしく、自分が臆病者だったことを思い知らされる。妻に対する気持ちはじつに微妙だ。また妻のほうもこの状況をどうしていいかわからないでいる。

　こんなマカンバー夫妻に、白人のガイド役ウィルソンが加わり、三人の気持ちが複雑に絡み合っていく。そして、次のハンティングが始まるのだが……。

　ヘミングウェイの作品というと、スポーツやハンティングやフィッシングの描写や、凄惨な戦場の描写が具体的で的確でリアルなので有名だが、登場人物の心理描写がそれ以上に魅力的だ。それはここに収録した２編を読んでもらえば十分に納得してもらえると思う。

　1933年、ヘミングウェイは妻のポーリーンのおじから多額の資金援助を受けてアフリカにサファリ旅行にでかけた。そのときの経験をもとに書かれたのがこの「キリマンジャロの雪」と「フランシス・マカンバーの短く幸せな生涯」（1938年に出版された『第五列と最初の四九の短編』（The Fifth Column and the First Forty-Nine Stories に収録）だ。それからもうひとつ『アフリカの緑の丘』（1935年出版）がある。こちらは回想録だが、これらの短編とはまた違った味わいがある。ぜひ読んでみてほしい。

金原瑞人

［著者］
アーネスト・ヘミングウェイ　Ernest Hemingway

アメリカの小説家（1899-1961）。イリノイ州オークパーク生まれ。高校卒業後新聞記者となる。第一次大戦やスペイン内乱での従軍経験をもとにした『武器よさらば』『誰がために鐘は鳴る』など、自身の実体験に取材した作品を多く残した。『老人と海』が世界的ベストセラーとなり、1954年ノーベル文学賞受賞。シンプルで力強い文体と冒険的なライフスタイルは20世紀のアメリカの象徴とみなされ、各方面に影響を与えた。

［編者］
金原瑞人（かねはら・みずひと）

法政大学教授、翻訳家。ヤングアダルト小説をはじめ海外文学の紹介、翻訳で著名。著書『翻訳のさじかげん』（ポプラ社）ほか。訳書『豚の死なない日』（ロバート・ニュートン・ペック、白水社）『青空のむこう』（アレックス・シアラー、求龍堂）『国のない男』（カート・ヴォネガット、ＮＨＫ出版）『月と六ペンス』（サマセット・モーム、新潮文庫）ほか多数。

金原瑞人 MY FAVORITES

キリマンジャロの雪 THE SNOWS OF KILIMANJARO /
フランシス・マカンバーの短く幸せな生涯
THE SHORT HAPPY LIFE OF FRANCIS MACOMBER

2014年 7月20日　第1刷発行
2023年10月31日　第2刷発行

著者　　アーネスト・ヘミングウェイ

編者　　金原瑞人

発行者　辻一三

発行所　株式会社 青灯社
東京都新宿区新宿 1-4-13
郵便番号 160-0022
電話 03-5368-6923（編集）
　　 03-5368-6550（販売）
URL http://www.seitosha-p.co.jp
振替　00120-8-260856

印刷・製本　モリモト印刷株式会社
© Mizuhito Kanehara 2014
Printed in Japan
ISBN978-4-86228-073-2 C0082

小社ロゴは、田中恭吉「ろうそく」（和歌山県立近代美術館所蔵）をもとに、菊地信義氏が作成

●青灯社の英語の本

英単語イメージハンドブック
定価 1800円 + 税

大西泰斗(東洋学園大学教授)

1冊で基本的な英単語のイメージがすべて分かる集大成。

英語世界の表現スタイル 〜「捉え方」の視点から

吉村公宏(奈良教育大学教授)　定価 1500円 + 税

英語圏では言いたいことから一直線に表現する方法を好む。日本人はうず潮型の表現を好むから海外で理解されにくい。

語源で覚える英単語 3600
定価 1700円 + 税

藤井俊勝(東北福祉大学教授)

接頭辞19種と語根200種の組み合わせで覚える、効率的な単語増強法。

金原瑞人 MY FAVORITES

金原瑞人氏の詳しい注つきで辞書なしに読む英語シリーズ。

征服されざる者・サナトリウム
THE UNCONQUERED / SANATORIUM　定価 1200円 + 税

サマセット・モーム著

THE BOX
定価 1200円 + 税

ブルース・コウヴィル著

英語圏で大人気の児童文学作家のやさしい短編。

変身 THE METAMORPHOSIS
定価 1200円 + 税

フランツ・カフカ著

異邦人 THE STRANGER
定価 1200円 + 税

アルベール・カミュ著